You're Not Dead 'til I Say You're Dead

A Nurse's Reflections on Death, Dying and the Near-Death Experience

By Joyce Victor, PhD, RN

NORTHAMPTON HOUSE PRESS

1/18

14.95

For PapaGino

Contents

Introduction:

By Dr. Brenda Hage, Ph.D., DNP, CRNP, Assistant Dean, College of Health Sciences and Education, Chief Nurse Administrator, Misericordia University

Throughout my 28 years of nursing and advanced practice, I've dealt with death many times. However, it's become much more real for me since my father developed fronto-temporal dementia and one of my adult children was diagnosed with brain cancer.

As a daughter and mother, I want to ensure that my loved ones are comfortable, free of pain and that their wishes for end of life are honored. As a clinician and caregiver, I know that to ensure this requires conversations that are sometimes uncomfortable and sad.

Too often we think we're sparing someone's feelings when in fact, it's our own discomfort we are trying to alleviate. By bringing up this difficult topic, there can be relief and empowerment for those we love when we talk honestly with them about what quality of life means to them and what their values about health, life, and death are. Many individuals express relief in being able to finally say out loud what they've been worrying about.

The CDC report *The State of Aging in America* (2013) indicates that the number of adults 65 and older is expected to reach 72 million or about 20% of the population by 2030. However, living longer doesn't necessarily mean living better. The rise in the incidence of multiple chronic conditions, changes in traditional family structure and support, and increasing health care costs have created a perfect storm for older adults. Death can also come too early to those in the prime of their lives.

According to data from a 2013 Pew Research Center survey report on end of life medical treatments, those in our country who have given significant thought about what they want in terms of end of life medical treatment comprise roughly one third (37%) of Americans. Almost the same number (35%), have documented their wishes in writing, but another 27% of the population has spent little or no time considering this issue. Although 80% of Americans would prefer to die at home, 60% die in acute care hospitals, 20% in nursing homes, and only about 20% actually die at home (Stanford School of Medicine, Palliative Care, 2017). The implications associated with this information are numerous. Health care professionals should be trained in how to engage in difficult conversations and properly document end of life care planning. Physician Orders for Life Sustaining Treatment (POLST©), is a national paradigm that began in Oregon used for end of life discussions and documentation that translates individuals' wishes into actionable medical orders. States need to develop interoperable registries for advanced directives, living wills, and POLST orders that can follow people as they travel and that are available to health care institutions and providers. Health care systems should adopt the POLST paradigm so that medical orders outlining end of life wishes on key areas including preferences for CPR and mechanical ventilation, tube feedings, IV fluids, antibiotics, and other interventions are immediately available at the point of care and on the electronic medical record in a timely way. POLST orders should also follow patients from one clinical setting to another and even home. Third party payers need to value the importance of end of life care planning and compensate providers for their time and services accordingly.

Let's begin to remove the stigma associated with talking about death and dying. Start The Conversation©, and Let's Have Dinner And Talk About Death, are examples of websites devoted to encouraging conversation about end of life.

Taking the sunrise view, end of life planning actually begins as early as sixteen, when teens decide whether or not to become organ donors on their driver's licenses. We must think about and plan for death just as we carefully plan for and celebrate birth, graduation, marriage and other milestones. In doing so, we can give "voice to our choices" and provide clarity during this challenging time and truly help people as they ease from one life plane to the next. One of the biggest gifts we can give to a loved one is to clearly share our wishes and plans for end of life. I've seen families split apart by not knowing what their loved ones' wishes were.

Not only should we document our end of life wishes, but we should also decide who our proxy decision maker should be in the event we cannot speak or decide for ourselves if we become incapacitated. A health care power of attorney can be appointed and this individual should be someone you trust, who will advocate for your wishes to be carried out, regardless of his or her personal feelings on the matter.

Sometimes those closest to us may not be able to do so and appointing another may be necessary. We not only want to live well, but we want to die well. In order to realize this goal, the necessary conversations, documentation, communication, and advocacy with the health care team must be done in advance.

Dr. Joyce Victor offers a candid and honest look at death and dying through her new work, *You're Not Dead 'til I Say You're Dead.* In her honest and refreshing style, she shares her stories of death and how these exposures have influenced her world view. Dr. Victor's passion for sharing her stories and lessons learned about death and dying is evident in every page. As she tells us, "They are very much alive as part of me. And as long as I keep their spirit with me, they will never be dead, until I say they are dead."

Those we love and have known may no longer be present in body, but their words and spirits remain with us still.

Going to Heaven!
I don't know when
Pray do not ask me how!
Indeed I'm too astonished
To think of answering you!
Going to Heaven!
How dim it sounds!
And yet it will be done
As sure as flocks go home at night
Unto the Shepherd's arm!

Perhaps you're going too!
Who knows?
If you should get there first
Save just a little place for me
Close to the two I lost –
The smallest "Robe" will fit me
And just a bit of "Crown" –
For you know we do not mind our dress
When we are going home –

I'm glad I don't believe it
For it'd stop my breath –
And I'd like to look a little more
At such a curious Earth!
I am glad they did believe it
Whom I have never found
Since the mighty autumn afternoon
I left them in the ground.

– from "Going To Heaven" by Emily Dickinson

Preface:
SO MANY QUESTIONS, SO LITTLE TIME

If a man has a cardiac arrest in the forest and there's no one around to pronounce him dead, *is* he dead?

When most people are driving to work, they think of things like, did I unplug the iron? I wonder if this meeting is going to be long. I hope that meat defrosts.

I'm driving to work thinking about death.

Lately, I've been thinking a lot about it. And I have a lot of questions. That's ironic, since just a few years ago, I thought I had all of the answers. I'm a registered nurse, after all; I'm supposed to.

Since childhood, I thought I'd understood death and I was never afraid of it. At camp and sleepover parties, at night, when the grownups went to sleep, we huddled in a tight circle and listened intently as the older girls told ghost stories and shared urban legends. They spoke with authority and we never questioned the authenticity of their tales.

Most nights, the stories frightened everyone to the point of sleeplessness. But the stories didn't scare me.

The older girls told us that if we went into a dark bathroom, held a flashlight to our chin, and said "Bloody Mary" three times while we looked into the mirror, we would see what we would look like when we were dead.

This secret information was usually whispered to us as we sat in a tight pack, hoping we wouldn't wake the counselors or parents – or the beetles that sometimes infected our cabins. Then the older girls dared us to try this crazy ritual.

"So," they said, as they scanned the mass of trembling bodies, "who's brave enough?"

There was a moment of hesitation from the group. "What's the matter? Are you all babies?"

The other girls squealed and gasped and clustered closer, but it didn't scare me. In fact, it made me curious. And I was the kid who always took their dares.

I stood, trotted through the shaking crowd, and pranced into the bathroom. I shut the door and stood alone in front of the mirror in the pitch-black room. I clicked on my flashlight and pressed it to my chin.

"Bloody Mary. Bloody Mary. Bloody Mary."

What I saw in the mirror at the end of this recitation was the same thing I'd seen at the beginning of it.

So, for those who still might think that if you do this crazy ritual, you'll see death looking back at you, it doesn't work. Unless of course, when I die, I am going to look like a nine year old holding a flashlight under my chin in a dark room. It sounds silly now but, as a child, this was part of the limited familiarity I had with the concept. I based my beliefs about and attitudes towards death on these rites of passage.

As a child, when I did have experiences with death, this fearless attitude always seemed to be the one I adopted. Was I just trying to impress the older kids? Did I think my courage would win me their respect? Was the brave facade just a coping mechanism?

I honestly don't know why I did it; but, when someone really died, I acted tough and pretended to handle it. By putting on this fearless front, I convinced myself Death was no big deal. Death didn't scare me.

As the years went on and my experiences with people passing away multiplied, I continued to put on this tough exterior, becoming more and more certain that the way I projected myself to the outside world was truly how I felt. Fake it until you become it, as they say. And by presenting a brave and unwavering front, I made others believe I wasn't afraid too. I convinced everyone that I understood the concept of mortality and could deal with it.

Maybe it's because I'm getting older (and, alas, closer to the end) but over the past few years, I've been thinking more objectively and seriously about death and how I really feel about it. Maybe it's because I made a job change to academia, and as I teach hopeful nursing students, I find myself questioning my entire career. But for some reason (or maybe for several reasons), when I think about death now, I *don't* understand it. I don't deal with it effectively. I'm afraid of it.

I've come to realize I have a lot of questions about death.

For instance, I wonder about the term *time of death*. As a nurse, I have written, said, and recorded that phrase too many times to count. It's just that now I've begun to question exactly what that term really means.

What is it that defines the moment of death? Is it when the heart stops beating? When the lungs stop moving air? Is it when the brain stops receiving signals from the ascending pathways, or when it stops sending out commands to the rest of the body? Does death not become official until someone in authority pronounces it like a decree, or writes it on a paper? Or is it not official until someone notifies the family?

I've seen hearts stop beating and then be restarted with defibrillators. I've seen mechanical ventilators push air into lungs unable to take it in themselves. I've seen patients live for years with minimal recordable brain function. I've seen people pronounced dead, and minutes later, they moved their arm or opened their eyes.

I have not only seen these things happen, but as a nurse for many years, I have helped them to happen. But now, looking back at my career, I've started to question everything I've done.

When I first began nursing school, the instructor asked each of us in the class why we wanted to be nurses. We all gave the same replies. We wanted to help people. We wanted to save lives. It wasn't until I was actively practicing nursing that it started to occur to me that saving a life doesn't necessarily mean helping someone.

As an adult, I now realize life is more than a beating heart and breathing. And death is more complex than an arrested heart and the absence of breathing.

Both are much more complex.

Life involves interaction with the world. It involves seeing, hearing, tasting, and feeling. It involves caring, loving, learning, and even worrying.

Life cannot just be defined by the flesh and the DNA that comprise what we are, but by the experiences and the spirit that made us who we are. Living involves both our physical being and our spirit, and thus, dying does too. In fact, every day that we live, we are twenty-four hours closer to death. So could it not be said that when we conceive we are living, we are in actuality dying?

And thus, living and dying are one and the same. They cannot be separated.

Experience has taught me that after a person is pronounced dead, his or her body continues to interact with its environment. There are even scientific terms for the processes: rigor mortis, algor mortis, and so on. So why is it so difficult to believe that the spirit continues to interact with its environment too?

The true difference, then, between life and death, is that the body and the spirit are no longer acting in unison. The body is decaying, but what the spirit is doing remains a mystery.

And, if I continue to hold on to the spirit of a person long after the body is gone, is that loved individual truly dead? Perhaps the "time of death" is not the moment the body is pronounced dead, but rather the moment I decide to let go of the spirit.

Solving the mystery of death and the spirit has been an unattainable goal for me. But I keep trying. And I've come to realize that while living and dying are just terms to identify a process, *being* alive and *being* dead are two distinctive states. How the two are defined may be different for each of us, and it may be different for each experience we have with death. For me to be able to define life and death for myself, I've come to the conclusion that I must think intimately about both living and dying.

As a nurse, the more I examine both my personal and professional experiences with dying, the more I learn about living. The more I reflect on my experiences with death, the more I come to value life. Not just the life of my body, but the life of my spirit. I suppose we all need to look to death for the lessons it can teach us about life.

Throughout my nursing career, I've had the privilege of seeing the fine line that separates life and death. There are times when death cedes to life and times when life cedes to death. Both are equally amazing.

Suddenly finding myself being middle-aged and no longer practicing nursing at the bedside, I've decided to explore my experiences with death in hopes of better understanding both death and life. My experiences have been garnered from over thirty years as a registered nurse and over fifty years as one of the living . . . or, given my latest hypothesis, maybe I should say, as one of the dying.

I've changed the names and a few details to protect those who have not yet passed on, as well as those who are not dead to me. However, these are all true stories, startling as some may seem. I'll tell them as my memory has preserved them. They are not chronological but linked, as memories trigger other memories.

I'll share them with you as honestly and openly as I can. Come along for the ride as I journey through my experiences with death. Though, given my driving record, it might be better if we walk through this one. . . .

Because I could not stop for Death —
He kindly stopped for me —
The Carriage held but just Ourselves –
And Immortality.

— from "Because I could not stop for Death" by
Emily Dickinson

One
BEEN THERE, DONE THAT:
My Near-Death Experience

The year was 1983. I was in my second semester of nursing school. I was young, but thought I was mature. I was naïve, but thought I was learned. I was mortal, but thought I was invincible.

Things could not have been better in my life. I was doing well in school. I was making friends. I'd found a whole new stock of boys at college. I was feeling pretty damn smug.

I'd taken college credits while still in high school, so while my classmates went to King's College for Anatomy and Physiology II, I went home and watched soap operas. When I met my friends again for Chemistry Lab, I would fill them in on the latest episode of *All My Children*. (At that time, it was vital for us to know what was going to happen to Jenny and Greg.)

It was the first day of March and the weather was unusually nice. The temperature was in the sixties. I was glad to put away my winter coat and boots and to wear my new Izod jacket and Zodiac shoes.

The accumulation of snow along the roadsides was melting before my eyes. Aldo Nova's "Fantasy" was playing on my car stereo. I loved that song. I turned it up louder. My foot tapped the floor near the clutch. My shoulders and head bobbed with the beat. I sang the lyric as I drove.

PennDOT had just added a new exit off Route 29 and for the past few weeks, I'd been taking it on my return trip home each day. I'm not sure it was any shorter than my old route, but it was new. I liked new.

There was a school bus in front of me and I was a tad annoyed it was going so slowly. Plus I couldn't see beyond it. When the bus stopped and put on its turn signal to go left, I tapped my thumb on the steering wheel to show my impatience. (To whom exactly I was showing it, I don't know.) And when the bus finally turned out of my path, I accelerated.

A rabbit hopped out from the roadside brush and onto the pavement. I yanked the wheel and swerved to the left. I found myself on the opposite side of the road with a car in the oncoming lane heading straight toward me. I jerked the wheel back and swerved to the right. The car crossed the roadway and the passenger side skidded over the curb and into the dirt. The front tire caught on the rugged gray stone that lined the roadside. I fought the wheel, trying desperately to get the tires back onto the macadam. But the passenger-side wheels failed to jump the curb and return to the road. They stayed in the dirt. I tried again to break free and get back in my lane. I panicked. I pushed my foot as hard as I could on the brake, but accidentally hit the gas instead. The car crashed into a utility pole. The steel hood buckled. The engine came to an abrupt halt. The pole cracked in half and fell onto the hood and roof.

I found myself in another dimension. I was out of my body. From wherever I was now, I could see my little gold car in the distance, on the side of the road. The hood looked like an upside down V. A pole was hanging over the roof. Its wires dangled above the car.

People stood around. They were looking inside. What were they were looking for? Somehow, it didn't register that they were looking at me (well, at least at my body). Then, for some reason, I decided I didn't care. I turned my back to them.

A breathtaking garden surrounded me. It was the type of garden one might see where there are acres of sprawling land. Wild, yet well-manicured.

I was walking in a large open field. I say I was walking, but I felt so light and carefree, it was more like floating. The grass beneath me was a blend of the most beautiful shades of green I had ever seen. It was spotted with patches of flowers. I call them flowers, but they were like nothing I'd seen before. It was as if a box of crayons had exploded into fireworks, making new, beautiful colors . . . colors that I was seeing for the very first time.

I felt wonderful. There was no pain or stress or worry. I was totally free. I loved the feeling and I frolicked through the garden like a child.

There was a path and I followed it. To my left was a grouping of trees. An awe-inspiring light gleamed from beyond them. I ran toward it.

But just before I reached the light, something stopped me. I don't know what. Just a force that stopped me. I stood near a rock to my left, staring into the light. There was a voice. A woman's voice. A soothing voice. I couldn't make out her words; yet for some inexplicable reason, I believed I understood what she was saying. I knew I needed to listen.

Perhaps she was giving me some sort of choice. Maybe she was telling me my fate, or giving me a warning. To this day, I have no idea what she actually said.

Other than this vision from the garden, I have only flashes of memories of the accident and the hours that followed.

I was sitting on the roadside, with a huddle of people around me. I can't remember what they looked like. I can't recall anything specific, just flashes.

"Don't touch your face," a man said in a kind voice. "The ambulance will be here soon."

Blackness.

"Do you have any identification?" someone asked.

Blackness.

"Take a deep breath and hold it."

I was in a machine. A woman in scrubs was standing nearby.

Blackness.

"Lie still."

I was lying on a stretcher. The walls were institutional green. They reminded me of the color of the pea soup my mom sometimes made for supper. There was a large round light above my head. It was not turned on.

Blackness.

"Do you know where we can reach your parents?"

Blackness.

I heard my mother's voice in the distance. I think she was crying.

Blackness.

"Can you tell us what happened?"

I don't know. I really don't know. I thought this. I don't know if I said it, but it was the truth.

A woman put her face close to mine. She was wearing a white lab coat. "I need to stitch up your lip." Her dark hair was pulled back. Loose curls framed her petite face and a small red dot was centered on the dark skin of her forehead. She had a thick accent. "I don't want to numb you. It will make it too hard to align the tissue."

I saw a curved needle with a long black thread coming toward my upper lip. The needle pierced the skin.

Blackness.

* * *

When I woke the following day, I ached everywhere. My pillow was covered with clumps of hair that had fallen out. I looked down at my legs. Skin was ripped open under each knee. Hues of purple and red were surfacing down each shin. My right hip throbbed. My head was pounding. I could feel the sutures beneath my nose.

My mother sat at my bedside.

"Is there a mirror here?" I asked.

"It's in the bathroom. You can't go. You have a concussion. You aren't allowed out of bed."

"Is there a mirror?" I asked the student nurse who was caring for my hospital roommate.

"Sure. It's right here in your over-bed tray." She slid a taupe plastic bin out and opened the lid.

"I look like Adolf Hitler." I slammed down the lid and slid the bin back into place.

"You're lucky to be alive," my mother said.

I turned on my side, away from her, and thought about the garden. I didn't feel lucky. I wanted to go back. But I didn't tell her about it. I didn't dispute her comment. I just lay on my side and thought it was nicer in the garden. I didn't have pain there. I didn't have scars.

* * *

As days and then weeks passed, I heard the phrase "You're lucky to be alive!" over and over. Each time, my mind went back to the garden. I couldn't tell anyone about it. They wouldn't have understood. They would have thought I was a freak. It was bad enough my face was messed up. I didn't want people thinking my brain was too.

I kept my vision to myself for years. But at night, when I was alone in my bed, I asked, why?

Why was I back here on this earth? I didn't have a logical answer, but I could hear her voice and I knew here was where I belonged, at least for the time being.

A child said *What is the grass?* fetching it to me with full hands.

How could I answer the child? I do not know what it is any more than he.

— from "Song of Myself" by Walt Whitman

Two
IT'S NOT ABOUT ME:
A Teenager's Lesson

I recall incidents of death in the years before I became a teenager, not really as isolated events, but as an amalgam of memories.

My mother would get a phone call. She stretched the cord of the mustard-yellow telephone over to the brown and orange Early-American style rocking chair. "That's terrible," she would say into the mouthpiece.

I didn't need to hear her words to know the news was not pleasant. Her bright hazel eyes were usually smiling, but when a call like this came in, they darkened. Her mouth dropped open a bit and stayed open, even when no words were coming out.

"When?"

After asking this, my mother sat silently, leaning forward. She stared at the brown plush carpet under her feet until she spoke again.

"Was he sick?"

She looked concerned. She sat erect, not allowing her spine to touch the back of the chair as it usually did when she was having a casual conversation.

The voice on the other end would be indiscernible. It reminded me of the phone conversations I heard in those

"Peanuts" television movies that aired every holiday season.

"When is the viewing?"

Waht waht waht waht waht waht was all I heard coming from the other end.

Then my mother ended the conversation and hung up. She continued about her daily chores until it was time to relay the news of the death to my father at the dinner table.

On some occasions, she and my father took my older sister and me along to the viewing. I'm not sure what the criteria were that made them decide whether or not we went; I just know, that every once in a while, we did.

I was probably around eight. We parked in the lot adjacent to the large white colonial-style building where my grandfather had had his viewing just a few years prior. Perhaps that's why even before I went in, I wasn't looking forward to my visit.

At the front entrance my father held the large white wooden door open for my mother, my sister and me. I could smell roses and cigarette smoke as soon as we got inside the dimly lit foyer. My mother wrote something in a book that lay open on a stand. Then she turned to my sister and me. She crouched down to our eye level and whispered, "When we get in there, kneel in front of the casket and say a prayer. Then when you go over to the family, tell them that you're sorry."

"Sorry!" My voice resounded inside the vaulted space. "For what? It's not my fault."

My mother cupped her hand over my mouth and gave me a stern look.

I knew better than to say another word. I followed her directions. I knelt in front of the casket. Once my knees sank into the soft padding, my eyes came level with the side of the coffin. I could barely see the stiff powdered skin of the corpse. I took a deep breath of the rose-scented air and said the short prayer the nuns had taught us at my school. "Eternal rest grant unto him oh Lord and let perpetual light shine upon him may his soul and all the souls of the faithfully departed through the mercy of God rest in peace amen."

It always came out in one long breath. I didn't know what some of those words meant, much less when they were strung together. But still, I did what I was told.

"I'm sorry." I repeated to each of the few family members standing in a line next to the casket. And when I got back into the car, I took the scolding.

"How embarrassing!" my mother reprimanded. Then she repeated what I'd said in the foyer for my father, even though he'd been standing there when I said it.

"Why do you always do that to us?" my father asked.

My mother didn't give me a chance to answer (not that I actually had an answer). "You should know better. Your father and I certainly set a better example than that for you. And you don't see your sister doing stuff like that. She listens."

They told me I should listen more than I talk. They told me I should be more respectful. They told me all about how sad these people were that the man in the casket had died.

I took it all in without understanding any of it. I didn't know this man. His death didn't affect me. I would still go to school. I would still have my friends. I would still listen to my David Cassidy albums when I got home. And I would still not understand why I was supposed to be sorry.

At least, that would be how it was until my teenage years. Then, without warning, my idea of death would change. I would learn why people said they were sorry at wakes and funerals.

We'd just finished the ninth grade when my best friend Lisa's mother died. At fourteen, I now understood that when someone died, it was permanent. I don't know how I knew this. It's not like one day someone sat me down and told me. But somehow I knew through my limited experience that when people died, they didn't come back.

No one ever told me how death affected others either. I'm sure they tried but somehow I never absorbed the concept. I looked at death only as it affected me.

No one ever shared feelings about death. Come to think of it, no one ever asked me about my feelings. But when my friend's mother died, I became suddenly aware the world did not revolve around me. I lost my narcissistic views. I became painfully aware that death did affect others, not just me. Other people's worlds were disrupted to an even greater extent than mine.

For me, this lesson was a painful one. And it came when I was still not prepared to deal with it. Was I supposed to act brave and hold back the tears? Was I supposed to brood and lock myself in my room crying? I really didn't know what people expected.

I remember Lisa telling me her mother had cancer but not really knowing what that meant. We simply talked about it like we talked about anything else: matter-of-factly. Karen got a green dress for the dance. The chain on my bike broke. Lisa's mother has cancer.

We had no experience with cancer and no one ever talked to us about it. But I remember how people looked at Lisa with pity when they heard. I can recall my family taking Lisa with us for pizza on a Friday night. We ran into one of their many acquaintances.

"You know our daughters," they said to their friend. "And this is Joyce's friend, Lisa." Then they added her last name with the sort of tone one would use when giving a hint.

"Oh," the friend replied with a sigh. Then she tilted her head and forced a grin with tight lips. Her eyes lacked the sparkle that usually came along with a smile.

What is with these people? I thought.

Perhaps at fourteen I lacked the awareness to associate cancer with death. I knew little about death and even less about cancer. I'd never known anyone with that disease before. If anyone I knew had cancer before that, no one ever mentioned it. No one ever talked about it with me. Terms like *chemotherapy* and *radiation* were new. Cancer came with no instructions. So for me, the meaning of those words was based solely on this one experience.

Chemotherapy meant Mrs. N would go away for a few days and come home vomiting. *Radiation* meant she would be tired and unable to get up from her recliner. I took these things in stride and although Mrs. N's appearance changed right before my eyes, I somehow didn't really notice the weight loss or thinning hair.

* * *

As best friends, Lisa and I spent every day together. We would ride our bikes, play tennis behind the elementary school and swim in the pool in my backyard. When we went to her house, things seemed pretty much the same. She and I would sit on the red shag carpeting in the family room with our legs folded in a lotus position, watching a small black and white television.

Video games were brand new and Lisa had a state of the art gaming system with joysticks that allowed us to play Pong (a very crude electronic version of ping pong). We would sit for hours maneuvering the white rectangular paddles up and down on the screen trying to hit a small square that bounced robotically between them. The game required little concentration, so we would talk through the entire match.

Mrs. N would sit on the black recliner near the window holding the newspaper or a magazine. We knew she wasn't really reading. She was listening to us. We could tell because she would laugh at our stories and roll her eyes when we would talk about how cute Joe was or how awful Ronnie had acted at the dance.

While our affairs seemed to go on unchanged, things were shifting. Mrs. N got thinner. Her blond hair was replaced by a similarly styled wig. Her trips for chemotherapy got longer and her fatigue kept her in a hospital bed. She was dying.

I don't remember if anyone told me this or I figured it out on my own, but I wasn't surprised when the phone rang early one summer morning. I was in bed but I immediately homed in on my mother's voice in the adjacent bedroom.

"Oh, I'm so sorry, honey. Wait. Let me get Joyce."

My mother didn't need to summon me. I got out of bed and raced into her room to grab the receiver. Lisa delivered the news through tears and asked if I could come and stay with her while her father went to a relative's house to pick up her brother.

My father drove me to Lisa's house even though it was within walking distance. When we arrived, I insisted he didn't need to come in. I wasn't sure how I was supposed to act, and I didn't want him realizing I was unprepared to deal with the situation. I wanted him to think I was mature. So he simply pulled up in front of the ranch-style house and watched from the car until I was inside.

Lisa swung open the screen door to let me in. Her long nails scratched along the wire of the screen as she allowed the door to slowly shut behind me. She and I were alone in her house.

We hugged and cried a bit and then made our way into the family room where we sat next to each other on the sofa. Lisa talked about the week before, when we hadn't had the chance to see each other much. Her mother had been in the hospital, and both she and her father had visited frequently. Her younger brother wasn't permitted in the hospital. I'm not sure if it was because he was only ten or because he had a genetic condition that altered his intellectual development. Regardless of the rationale, he'd spent the prior week with relatives.

I don't know if a long period passed, but it seemed like forever as we sat there on the black and white velvet couch in the paneled family room. Neither of us really knew what to do. We cried and then we laughed and then we just sat and talked about the things we always talked about: the upcoming school year, cute boys and our other friends. How odd it seemed to be sitting there without hearing Lisa's mother's voice in our conversations. Every now and then I would find myself looking over at the empty chair near the window. I found myself longing to hear Mrs. N say that we were silly or see her trying to hold in her laughter when we would talk seriously about what type of gowns the bridesmaids would wear in our weddings. We never considered that velvet gowns in rainbow tones would be totally out-of-style long before either Lisa or I would be walking down the aisle.

Should we have cried? Laughed? Should we have called our other friends and told them what had happened? Should we have just sat in silence?

We did all of those things. We didn't know if they were wrong or right, but we did them because, quite honestly, we didn't know what else to do.

Sometime later that morning, we heard Mr. N's car pulling up in the driveway. The doors opened and closed. Two different doors. One for Lisa's dad. One for Lisa's brother. Open. Open. Close. Close.

Then there was a moment of quiet before the screen door handle clicked. The door swung open and my best friend's younger brother, Jake, burst in. His short blond hair highlighted his full face. His low-set eyes gleamed. His full lips curved into a bright smile as he yelled out, "Mommy!"

I felt helpless.

Jake looked at the empty recliner. His mother wasn't there. He looked at his sister and then at me and then back at his sister. "Where's Mommy?" He bounced his knees and patted the air in excitement. "They said she's not in the hospital anymore!"

Neither of us answered him. I felt pinned against the cushions of the couch, unable to move. I was afraid to cry. Lisa stared at her father who had come in a few steps behind her brother. Her big brown eyes looked glossy as tears formed.

Her father didn't look back to her. He simply walked closer to his son, took his hand, and led him past us. They walked into the kitchen and then disappeared from our view as they made their way into Mr. and Mrs. N's bedroom.

Lisa and I were once again alone in the family room. Neither of us spoke as we sat close to each other on the sofa. The house seemed exceptionally quiet. The clock on the wall above my head counted each second with a click and an echo.

Tick-ck. Tick-ck. Tick-ck. Tick-ck. Tick-ck. Tick-ck.

The world was passing in slow motion until we heard the squeak of the bedroom door being opened. Within seconds, Jake was back.

His legs seemed to drag as he approached us. His arms swung heavily at his sides. His eyes were rimmed with red and tears poured down his cheeks. He sobbed loudly. He looked at his sister and then at me. He looked at us again.

"Why did God take my mommy?" he wailed.

We both embraced him and cried along with him.

At fourteen, I had nothing to offer but a loving embrace that camouflaged the fact that I didn't have the answers.

I thought that maybe as I got older, things would make sense. I thought that perhaps at forty, I would have all the answers I pretended to have at fourteen.

Now I'm older than my parents were when Lisa and I were fourteen. What would I do if I were in the same situation as they were? What would I say to my child? Thinking about it only makes me realize that answers about death don't come to us as we age. Rather, more questions arise.

If I can stop one Heart from breaking
I shall not live in vain
If I can ease one Life the Aching
Or cool one Pain

Or help one fainting Robin
Unto his Nest again
I shall not live in vain.

– from "If I Can Stop One Heart From Breaking" by Emily Dickinson

Three
YOU ALWAYS REMEMBER YOUR FIRST:
Death and the Student Nurse

When I was young, people would ask, "What do you want to be when you grow up?"

My reply would change depending on the occasion. Replies varied from a physician to a make-up artist. But somehow when I pictured myself as an adult, I had a vision of being an English teacher. So it did make me wonder how I ended up being a registered nurse.

But over the years I came to realize that on an unconscious level, I'd always had a desire to help people and save lives. And, well, let's face it, no one ever died from a dangling participle (at least not that I ever heard of).

In my younger days, I began to understand why, when it came to dealing with death and dying, I put on a stoic front. On the outside, I was acting as though I accepted death, but on the inside, I was developing a determination to make a difference in the lives of those who were dying and of those who would go on living, as well.

I knew I couldn't change the past. I couldn't bring back the dead; but somehow, I thought I could make a difference in the future. Perhaps I rationalized that nursing would give me some sort of control, and that that control would cancel out the helplessness I felt in dealing with death and dying.

I went into nursing with aspirations of finding a cure for cancer or being lauded as a hero for rescuing a small child from some peril. But when school commenced, there was no lecture about the treatments for cancer. No one was teaching me rescue skills. In fact, the first semester was unlike anything I'd imagined at all.

The old red brick school building sat atop a hill next to another old brick building that had once been a hospital. At the time, much of the latter was abandoned, but a section was being used by a trucking company. Although the trucks couldn't be seen, the noise often disrupted lectures.

Some days, the students would go to one of the local colleges for classes on Anatomy & Physiology, Microbiology, and Chemistry. Other days, professors from the college would come to our school and teach Sociology and Psychology. But most days, I was cooped up in a small classroom with worn-out brown carpeting and dingy walls the color of urine. My classmates and I sat in uncomfortable wooden chairs positioned so closely we would bump elbows as we tried to write notes.

One of the instructors (who appeared to be as old as the building, if not older) sat at the front of the room on a desk with a plywood podium in front of her. From her perch, she read the *Fundamentals of Nursing* book to us.

I could have read it myself, but attendance was mandatory, so I sat in my assigned seat in the last row and tried to stay alert enough to follow along with her. Occasionally, I would take the cap off of my yellow highlighter. (No, I didn't sniff it.) I would highlight a word or sentence or paragraph. It wasn't that I thought the words were important. It was just something to do so I wouldn't fall to sleep.

When are we going to get to the good stuff? I would wonder. Please tell me there's more to nursing than this!

After a few weeks, I finally got a chance to do something that made me feel like a nurse. I got to give my assigned student partner a bed bath. And when I got it right, I was able to move on to counting my partner's pulse, taking my partner's temperature and measuring my partner's blood pressure. Once I showed I could perform these tasks proficiently, I could try them out on real patients. That's how nursing school worked. Practice on your classmates. And if you do it right, you can go to the hospital and do it for real.

Our first clinical rotation at the hospital began six weeks into the semester. We were divided into groups. Each group was then assigned to a particular medical-surgical unit at our affiliated hospital. When the first day of the clinical experience came, I was to arrive on the sixth-floor nursing unit before the 7:00 a.m. shift began.

It was my first clinical experience as a nursing student and I was excited. It was like getting ready for the first day of school all over again. I woke early and donned my powder blue dress with the Peter Pan collar and the neatly pressed white apron over it. I wore new white stockings and clean white shoes. I filled my pockets with new silver bandage scissors, a notepad, and pen (one of those clicker kind that could write in four different colors). As I carried my white student nurse's cap in its clear plastic case into the hospital, I thought about the lives I would save.

A white sheet of paper was hanging at the sixth floor nurses' station. It listed the name of each student in my group. After each name was a patient assignment. I glided my finger down the sheet. It shook as I ran it over the names. Annette. Marianne. Lisa. I continued down until I found my name. It was second from the bottom. With my new pen, I wrote down the patient's name on the first sheet of my notepad. Then I walked over to get the chart from the chart rack.

There was a sticker on the front with III printed in black marker. Flipping through the chart, I saw the same III at the top of each page.

"What does this roman numeral three mean on all of the sheets?" I asked one of the registered nurses who worked on that unit.

"It means the patient is a code level three."

The nurse must have seen me shrug and crinkle my nose. I didn't understand.

"It means that when she dies, she doesn't want to be resuscitated," she explained.

"Oh. So if she dies, she doesn't want anyone to do CPR?"

"Right." The registered nurse peered over the top of the chart I was holding and read the patient's name. "Is she your patient?"

I nodded.

"She's actively dying. She'll probably die for you today."

The nurse's tone made this sound like a good thing, but my eyes opened so wide I'm sure she could see the white of my corneas around my bluish gray irises. What about saving people? I wanted to ask. Instead, I stood there staring for a moment before I finally managed to get a few words out. "What am I supposed to do?" I was petrified.

"You stay with her, so she doesn't have to be alone when she passes." The nurse cocked her head and smiled without showing her teeth. Then she patted me lightly on the shoulder and went back to whatever she'd been doing before I interrupted her.

I felt disappointed. I wondered if my instructor didn't trust me. Maybe she thought I didn't know what I was doing so she had given me a dying patient. This way if I messed up she could just say, "Oh well, she was dying anyway."

Thinking the instructor was lacking confidence in my abilities saddened me at first, but then I was determined to prove her wrong. Looking through the chart, I was hopeful to find something I could write in my notebook, something that I could say or do to make my instructor proud of me. All I managed to scribble was the patient's name, her room number, her age and her doctor's name before it was time for our preclinical conference with our instructor, Mrs. C.

I joined the other students in the spacious lounge area at the end of the hallway and took a seat on one of the blue chairs. Not in the mood to talk about my patient assignment, I listened as the others chattered excitedly about theirs. When our instructor entered, we were silent.

Mrs. C welcomed us to clinical and told us a bit about how the day would be organized. I could barely concentrate on what she was saying. My mind was too preoccupied with my patient. I was having visions of walking in my assigned room and seeing an embalmed body in a casket. I tried to push aside visions of an old stiff and wrinkled body clad in some silky pink negligee. I had to focus on my instructor. She was asking each of us to tell her a little bit about our assigned patient before we would go out onto the nursing unit to start our patient care.

I forced myself to listen as students talked about dressings and tubes that their patients had and asked questions about what seemed, at the time, to be complicated procedures. Mrs. C answered them and assured them that she would be right there to help.

When my turn came, all I could offer was what I had written in my notebook, followed by a lame, "She's a code level three."

"And what does that mean, 'code level three'?" my instructor asked.

I told her what the nurse had told me.

"Very good." She smiled at me and nodded as though I'd just offered an explanation of brain surgery.

A perplexed expression was all I could offer back. "What am I supposed to do if she dies?"

Mrs. C leaned her ample body forward. Her tone seemed matter-of-fact. "Post mortem care." Each word and syllable was deliberate.

My jaw opened, but no sound came out.

Her chubby cheeks turned pink as they puffed out with laughter. "Just come and get me," she finally offered after regaining her composure and smoothing back a few strands of gray hair that had fallen from her tight bun.

I looked around at my fellow students. They were all gaping. In my head, I could hear them thinking. *Poor Joyce. Her patient's going to die.*

I returned my attention to my notebook as Mrs. C called on another student. And when she'd heard from each of us, she sent us out onto the unit to begin our shift.

* * *

My body felt tight as I took each step through the wide hallway that lead from the conference room, past the nurses' station and into the patient area. I looked at room numbers printed in white block letters on squares of brown plastic and mounted to the right of each doorway. Room 612 was the second door on the right.

"Here goes," I mumbled to myself. I took a deep breath and stood in the doorway. The patient was lying still in the bed and I stared for a moment. Taking a step closer, I watched her chest rise and fall with each shallow breath.

Another step closer and I adjusted the gold watch on my left wrist. Another step. Then I counted her respiratory rate.

One breath. Two breaths. Three breaths. Four. Five. Six. Seven breaths.

I pulled the notepad out of my apron pocket and neatly printed *Resps* = 7 in blue ink on an empty white page.

One more step and my apron brushed the side rail of the bed. I gently took the patient's arm. I wrapped my fingers around her thin wrist and counted her pulse. She looked as though she was just sleeping. I began to relax and felt more confident as I checked the blood pressure and temperature. Then I recorded all of my findings, first in my notepad and then in the patient's chart.

"There," I told myself, "that wasn't so bad." The patient and I had both survived our first encounter.

Convincing myself that I should proceed as though she weren't dying, I began to give her a complete bed bath. In the oak cabinet next to her bed was a yellow rectangular basin. I filled it with warm water from the bathroom sink and took it over to her bedside. With a soft white washcloth, I washed her eyes and face. Just like they taught us at the school, I washed her arm from the fingers to the armpit and her legs from the thigh to the toes. And although I didn't know whether or not she could hear me, I narrated my actions to her as I proceeded.

"I'm just going to turn you on your side and wash your back now."

Each body part was washed and dried just as it was supposed to be. And when the bath was finished, I combed her hair, changed the linens on her bed, and made sure she looked comfortable.

It felt good to have accomplished something, but with four hours left to my shift, I stood staring at her, wondering what to do next. So I counted the patient's breaths again.

One breath. Two.

It seemed that each was more of an exhalation than anything else.

Three breaths.

I could barely see her take air in. She just pursed her lips and let out a little "puh."

Four breaths. Five breaths.

I noted the time and recorded my findings in my notepad.

Resps = 5, I printed.

I put the notepad back in my apron and looked around for something else to do. I straightened up, making sure all of the old linens were removed and properly placed in the laundry bin out in the hallway. I rearranged the few items I found on her bedside stand. I refilled her water pitcher with fresh water, even though I knew she wasn't able to drink it.

Over the next two hours, I counted her breaths again, and again, and again, until finally, there were none to count. I took her wrist. There was no pulse. I tried the carotid artery in her neck, but there was no pulse to be felt there either, so I returned my attention to her arm. I moved my fingers around her wrist and tried again to find a pulse. There was none, but I held on to her wrist anyway. I slid my hand down under her thin crooked fingers. I stood next to her and held her hand for a few moments.

Her skin was still warm and soft. It wasn't at all like the other dead bodies I'd touched in the past. She didn't look or feel like those I'd seen and touched at funeral homes.

I had to remind myself I'd never seen anyone die before. I'd only heard of them dying. By the time I saw them, they'd been removed from the hospital, refrigerated and embalmed.

It was somehow comforting to see that my patient, now dead, seemed not much different than she'd been when alive. I ran my hand over her soft wrinkled skin. I studied her, trying to note how she looked and how she felt. I tried to decipher what had changed in that moment between life and death. It didn't seem like much.

I gently placed her arm at her side. Then I went to find my instructor.

Over the years, I've found myself reminiscing about that first day of clinical and that first experience with dying. I faced it. I did it. And I felt content at the end of the day. It was the first time it had occurred to me that helping people and saving lives were not one and the same.

My idea of death was altered. I no longer envisioned Death as this mean intruder who snatched people away from their lives. Instead, She could be a peaceful visitor who left as quietly as She came.

We noticed smallest things
Things overlooked before
By this great light upon our minds
Italicized – as 'twere.

– from "The Last Night That She Lived" by Emily Dickinson

Four
LIFE AND DEATH SITUATIONS:
The Gray Area Between Life and Death

I spent many years trying to keep to the facts. To fit life and death into a theoretical framework. I was fascinated with books about death, especially ones that proposed theories and models.

In 1969, Elisabeth Kübler-Ross released the groundbreaking book, *On Death and Dying*. In it, Kübler-Ross posited five stages of grief: denial, anger, bargaining, depression and acceptance. The book was inspired by her work with terminally ill patients. I was just learning to read at the time her book was released, but have since read it many times, along with her other works.

I became interested in Kübler-Ross—not just her books, but in her. What was she like? Was she as fascinated with death as I was? Perhaps we had things in common. So, I not only read her books, I read about her and her life.

She was born in Switzerland, the first of female triplets. Coming to the United States, she entered medical school. It was there that she became perplexed by the treatment of terminally ill patients. She conducted a series of interviews with and observations of dying patients with a goal of describing the emotional processes they would progress through in order to come to terms with dying.

On Death and Dying described the stages of grief as a continuum of emotional phases a person proceeded through when he or she received a terminal diagnosis. Kübler-Ross suggested that the dying patient would go through each of the stages, beginning with denial and ending with acceptance.

These stages are well-known and are often woven into the story lines of movies and TV shows. Sometimes they're used to add reality to a drama. At other times, they're employed for comedic effect, as in one episode of *The Simpsons*, when Homer accidentally ate a poisonous blowfish and went through the five stages of grief in record time.

Dr. Kübler-Ross's research continued until her death in 2004. Her work expanded beyond dying and into the afterlife. She was fascinated with near-death experiences and communication with the dead through mediums. Although the original stages of grief have made their way into the mainstream since the publication of *On Death and Dying*, her theory has been remodeled several times since.

One of the first transformations originated with David Kessler, a thanatologist (the official term for a person who studies death and dying). He worked closely with Kübler-Ross. Together, they rewrote her theory as the stages of loss, rather than the stages of grief, with the focus on the emotional journeys experienced by the survivors. Their book, *On Grief and Grieving: Finding the Meaning of Grief Through the Five Stages of Loss* was published shortly after Kübler-Ross's death. That volume, like *On Death and Dying*, included interviews and observations. But this time, Kübler-Ross and Kessler changed their focus from the patient to those who were left behind, including family and friends, as well as the health care providers who attended to the dying.

A second transformation of the Kübler-Ross model was the realization that the stages of loss were not linear. The dying and the survivors do not always move through the stages in order. Completion of one stage does not mean the griever will not return to that stage. In fact, the opposite is true. Even those who've reached acceptance don't stay there. Instead, the person moves back and forth between these distinct emotional stages. The transition between the stages is not based on any logical order, but rather on the person's immersion in life. One may have come to accept a loss, only to be catapulted back into depression or anger based on a memory or experience.

Also, there is no relationship between the length of the dying process and the ability to transition through the stages of grief. It was originally thought that if the dying and the surviving had a longer time to prepare, they would move through the stages of grief and come to acceptance. This implies that a time will come when one is ready to die and the loved one is ready to let go. This is not true. The length of the dying process is not proportional either directly or indirectly to the grieving process. So in a prolonged dying, the grieving process for the survivor is neither shorter nor longer than with a sudden death. In fact, it seems that the grieving process that accompanies loss may actually *never* be over.

Grieving a loss is also not always dependent on the type of relationship shared by the dead and the living, nor is it related to the amount of time the surviving had known the deceased.

It seems that as time went on, Kübler-Ross realized there is no black and white to grieving. There is no black and white to death and dying. There are just shades of gray that people meander through.

If there is no black and white to death, then it may follow that there is no black and white to life. Thinking about death makes one think about life. If one questions when a person is officially dead, one must also question when a person is officially alive. Does life start at the moment of conception? Twenty weeks into gestation? At birth?

One thing I find interesting is that Kübler-Ross experienced several miscarriages prior to giving birth to two children. These miscarriages preceded the publication of *On Death and Dying* and I can't help but wonder if she saw any similarities between her journey through miscarriage and the emotions her research subjects shared with her on their journeys through dying. Unfortunately, I never had the privilege of meeting Kübler-Ross and have no way to know. But I do know many people who've had miscarriages and witnessed their emotional journeys. Each experience with miscarriage is as unique as each experience with death.

* * *

Back in the 1980s and 1990s, my group of friends was in that phase of life when every social gathering centered on conversations about proposals, wedding venues, and baby names. When someone was getting married, all the coworkers wanted to be there. When someone was having a baby, everyone wanted to go to the shower or visit the new parents as soon as they came home from the hospital.

As nurses, pregnancy was not something that could be kept a secret. Nurses are exposed to patients with all types of infections. We lift and turn patients who are sometimes two to three times our own weight. If someone was pregnant, she needed to let us know. Even a nurse who thought she *might* be pregnant would notify her coworkers of the possibility, so she would get an appropriate assignment.

I was not in a serious relationship, so I lived vicariously through my coworkers who were. Amy, a coworker I became close with, had just gotten married at the time we met. I remember the day she came into the small conference room where we assembled that morning to receive patient reports from the night shift staff. Another friend and coworker, Claire, was pouring coffee from our Mr. Coffee machine, which sat on a small end table under a window at the far end of the room. She handed me a mug of freshly brewed, caffeine rich liquid and I added creamer. Claire poured another mug and handed it to Amy.

Amy declined it and said she was going to make a pot of decaf once the regular was gone. We all stared at her as though she was refusing a million dollars. What nurse chooses decaf over regular before 7 a.m.?

Claire passed the mug to another coworker and bluntly asked what we were all thinking. "What? Are you pregnant?"

Amy grinned, "Yes."

Oohs and aahs delayed our change of shift report. We were all excited for Amy and bombarded her with the usual questions.

"When are you due?"

"Are you going to find out what you're having?"

"Is Steve excited?"

Every question was answered with "I don't know." She explained that she'd taken a home pregnancy test just that morning and she was still adjusting to the positive result. Her plan was to have our lab technician draw blood for a more official test, but she felt we should all know so we didn't think she was sneaking off to the lab to avoid work or being choosy about her patient assignment. She was always conscientious.

No one minded covering for her while she went to have blood drawn, and we were more than cautious assigning her patient care duties. After the blood work confirmed the pregnancy, Claire and I insisted on assisting all of her patients from bed to chair or chair to bed and bed to stretcher and stretcher to bed.

"We've got this. You relax."

"I'm having a baby, not a heart attack," she replied.

This went on for weeks, as did our enthusiastic conversations about whether she wanted a boy or girl (she didn't care as long as it was healthy), if she planned to nurse or bottle-feed (she planned to nurse), and what names she'd chosen (Jane for a girl and James for a boy).

Nearly two months later, as we came into report as usual, our head nurse entered with shoulders slumped. Her hands clenched the lapels of her white lab coat. Her eyelids drooped. Her lips were rolled inward and barely visible.

"What's wrong?" one of us asked.

"Amy called in sick."

We looked at her hoping Amy just felt tired. The first trimester had ended and perhaps the second was harder on her. We knew this was not typical in pregnancy, but we tried to be optimistic.

"She was spotting this morning and her doctor put her on bed rest."

Claire and I chatted all day, our words filled with worry about our friend and her baby. We called Amy when we were on our first break and she sounded hopeful. When our shift ended, we stopped by her apartment to check on her. She was wearing pajamas and sitting on a blanket in the middle of the floor watching television. She still seemed cheerful and assured us the spotting had eased up. She told us she was going to see her doctor the following day. "So don't worry when I'm not at work tomorrow."

We gave her hugs and told her we would be thinking of her. She said she would keep us posted.

Two days later, she was at work on a regular assignment.

"Are you okay?" I asked.

"We'll just have to try again," she answered.

I could see she was trying hard to not cry. I didn't know what else to say so I talked about work, as did everyone else. And Amy seemed to appreciate that. As the days passed, her bubbly, optimistic personality returned.

It wasn't until two months later that things changed. We ended our shift by giving report to the evening shift nurses. At the end of report, Kate, one of the second shift crew, asked us if we heard the news: "Roz is pregnant."

Amy appeared excited but as we left the hospital and walked to our cars, her eyes filled with tears. Without her saying a word, I could imagine the conversation inside her head:

I'm happy for Roz, said Amy's denial.

I just wish I were still pregnant too. I would be over halfway through by now, her depression lamented.

Roz didn't even want kids! her anger interrupted.

Maybe if I stop thinking about it, I will get pregnant again, bargaining added.

Acceptance was nowhere to be found as she moved through grieving's shades of gray.

* * *

Amy eventually had four children. Although I haven't seen her in years, Claire ran into her at the mall one day. Amy had two of her children with her.

They reminisced about the past when we were all coworkers with no children – just dreams of having them. They talked about the struggles of trying to get pregnant and trying NOT to get pregnant. They talked about the irony of Amy's first pregnancy ending in a miscarriage and her now having four children.

"They're getting so big," Claire said.

Amy looked at them lovingly and sighed. "The one I miscarried would have been 21 this year. Isn't that something?"

To Amy, her baby was alive from the moment she saw the positive home pregnancy test. And since he or she had lived, her baby also died. And she grieved the loss.

But that is not so for everyone.

* * *

Years later, I was working in the emergency department of another hospital. A woman came in complaining of abdominal pain and bleeding. We drew blood and did an ultrasound. She was approximately 18 weeks pregnant and was in the process of a spontaneous abortion, or miscarriage as it is more commonly known.

My coworker, Danielle, was assigned to the patient. A blue pad (or as we called it – a chuck) was placed under the patient and Danielle checked the pad frequently to monitor the bleeding. After a short time in the emergency room, the fetus was expelled onto the pad. Danielle slid the tiny lifeless fetus into a small stainless steel basin.

She took the basin into an empty bay and furtively called the rest of the emergency room staff in. "Look at this." She set it on a table. "It has little fingers and toes."

We all stood around the basin staring at the pink fetus inside. It was like a miniature newborn, with a round protruding belly and an umbilical cord connected to a small placenta. Of course, none of us cared about the placenta. We were fascinated with the baby. The fetus had a tiny head and tiny hands and feet. I'd never seen anything like it.

"What are we supposed to do with it?" one of the nurses asked.

Danielle explained that we needed to send it to the laboratory. There, they would check the blood type. They would examine the fetus and placenta for any missing pieces that might have been retained in the mother's uterus, or womb. "Of course, we have to wait to see what the mother wants to do."

Dr. T was the ER physician that day. He joined us in the bay. His tall, thin body hunched over the basin as he stood silent with his hands hidden in the pockets of his long white lab coat. He looked down but his gaze seemed distant. Having worked with him many times, I imagined he was running through pages of medical books, trying to create an algorithm on how to handle all of the possibilities this particular situation presented. He nodded to Danielle. "Guess I better go talk to her."

He left us and walked over to the bay where the woman was lying on a stretcher, still seemingly in shock over the cause of her belly pains. We followed but hung back, away from the bed, so we didn't overwhelm the patient.

The physician explained to the patient and to those of us still with him, that in Pennsylvania, the law stated that before the 16th week of pregnancy, a fetus wasn't considered viable. Nothing would need to be done but record the incident as a miscarriage.

He also explained that the law stated that after the 20th week, the fetus was considered viable. In this case, the baby would be considered "still born." Meaning that it was not miscarried, but born dead. A birth certificate and death certificate would both need to be generated.

In this particular patient's case, the fetus was at 18 weeks' gestation and fell into neither category. The law allowed the decision to rest with the woman. She had the choice to consider this incident a miscarriage or a stillbirth.

The physician also explained that she would have to have a procedure called a Dilation and Curettage, more familiarly known as a D and C. This would scrape the lining inside the uterus to remove any remnants of the placenta. She would have to follow up with a gynecologist to schedule that procedure.

The woman said she understood and, with no hesitation, chose the miscarriage. She didn't consider the baby to have ever been alive. She didn't even know she was pregnant. She did not want to name the baby or have a birth certificate prepared, nor did she want to bury it or have a death certificate prepared. She simply signed the forms releasing the fetus to the lab. She got dressed and left.

I saw no signs of anger or depression. There was no bargaining – just acceptance that she'd been unknowingly pregnant and had a miscarriage.

* * *

I often think about those two experiences. There were no clear answers. There was no right or wrong. There was no black or white. Everything was just some shade of gray.

* * *

Each time abortion becomes a political issue at election time, I think about that spontaneous abortion and miscarriage. I think about the little body in the basin. I remember Amy, and question my own beliefs. I wonder how there can be people out there who seem so steadfast in their convictions. They are so adamant that they know all about the beginning and ending of life.

Unlike them, I doubt. I question. When does our human existence begin? When does it really end? Do these people really have all the answers? Do they know something I do not? Once again, I find myself with more questions than answers.

NAY, do not dream, designer dark,

Thou hast portray'd or hit thy theme entire:

I, hoverer of late by this dark valley, by its confines, having glimpses of it,

Here enter lists with thee, claiming my right to make a symbol too.

For I have seen many wounded soldiers die,

After dread suffering—have seen their lives pass off with smiles;

And I have watch'd the death-hours of the old; and seen the infant die;

The rich, with all his nurses and his doctors;

And then the poor, in meagreness and poverty;

And I myself for long, O Death, have breathed my every breath

Amid the nearness and the silent thought of thee.

– from "Death's Valley" by Walt Whitman

Five
GOOD VERSUS EVIL:
When Death Is Not Peaceful

I grew up watching TV shows like *Dark Shadows*, reading books like *Carrie,* and seeing movies like *The Exorcis*t. So I didn't think I was afraid of anything. These creations were fiction. They were fake. Things happening on those shows didn't actually happen in the real world. Vampires didn't live in nearby mansions and none of my classmates had telepathic powers.

But I wasn't quite sure what I thought about ghosts and spirits. I'd never seen anyone who was possessed, though I sometimes wondered what possessed some of the boys in my grade school to do the things they did. I still wonder what goes through the mind of the opposite sex – but that is a whole different story!

I went to a Catholic elementary school. There, the nuns convinced us that there were demons all around trying to tempt us into a life of evil. So evil spirits did seem like a plausible explanation for some of the things I'd seen. But I wasn't buying the idea of people becoming possessed or needing exorcisms.

My sister claimed she'd seen my grandfather's ghost. So I figured if there were ghosts and spirits in our midst, they were probably friendly and intended no harm.

I'd heard talk about folks who spoke to dead relatives in their own dying process. People would often say their dead father had come to get their mother right before she died.

For example, my sister's neighbor Frank was scheduled for elective surgery. The morning he left for the hospital, my sister spoke to him. He told her his deceased mother had come to him the night before and invited him to join her.

My sister was upset by this, but reminded herself that Frank was only in his fifties and was in good health. When she heard he was out of surgery and doing well, she was relieved. But two days later, she received the news of Frank's death. He had developed a massive and fatal blood clot in his lungs (a pulmonary embolism, or simply PE).

I wondered if his mother had come back again. Perhaps she'd offered him another invitation. Maybe, on her second visit, she'd come with his other deceased loved ones. And this time, he'd decided to join them.

Perhaps when I was dying, all my family, and friends, who'd gone before, would be standing in a big group at Heaven's gate to greet me. That didn't sound scary at all. In fact, it sounded nice. Positive. Reassuring.

* * *

By my mid-twenties, I'd seen enough people die to feel confident that it was a peaceful process. Sure, illness could cause suffering but once a person was dying, he seemed to find some sort of inner peace.

As they died, their muscles relaxed and their efforts to breathe eased. The process seemed serene. At least that was my experience up until one day in the intensive care unit.

When I came to work that day, I was happy to be working with my friends on the day shift. I often rotated shifts and although I got along with all my coworkers, I was closest with the day nurses. We were friends outside of work.

On the day shift, the ICU was usually staffed with four nurses. But thanks to vacant positions and staff calling in sick, we were short that day. There were only three of us for seven critical patients.

Amy said she would take the desk and the patient in room seven. This meant she'd be in charge for the day and have a lighter patient assignment. Susie and I would split the remaining six beds, but we would all help each other as necessary.

While Amy went to the desk to review the charts, run and read EKG strips, and prepare paperwork for the diagnostic studies, Susie and I went from bed to bed taking vital signs, performing assessments, setting up patients for morning care and breakfast, and passing out linen for baths and bed changes.

I was at the bed of Miss Z, in room six, when something seemed off. According to the report, she'd been admitted the prior evening. She was diagnosed with alcoholism and was bleeding internally from ruptured diverticuli. This was a diagnosis not uncommon in alcoholics. Small areas of the bowel would begin bleeding and the body would not be able to stop it, since some of the substances needed to clot the blood are produced in the liver. That organ does not function properly when it's damaged through long-term excessive alcohol consumption.

Miss Z was not a candidate for surgery. If her blood couldn't clot, she would bleed to death in the operating room. So instead, we were treating her with medications to stop the bleeding and an intravenous (IV) to replace the fluids she was losing. She'd received a transfusion during the night to try to replace any blood she'd lost so far.

When Susie placed the sphygmomonometer's cuff (more commonly known as a blood pressure cuff) on her arm, Miss Z sprang up from her reclining position and let out a blood-curdling scream. Susie and I both jumped back. Miss Z stared up at a spot at the foot of her bed. "Noooooo!" she screamed.

It was as if she were looking at and speaking directly to someone, but there was nobody there.

Susie and I glanced at each other. "That just gave me goose bumps," I said.

"Me too! What the heck just happened?"

I shrugged. I didn't know and I couldn't explain it.

Miss Z sank back into the mattress of her bed and seemed to calm down. Susie and I assessed her as quickly as possible then ran to the desk to tell Amy about our encounter.

"You guys are joking around."

Sure, we had been known to pull pranks on each other from time to time, but this was not one of those times. "Seriously," I continued. "Her nose was all pointy and she looked terrified."

Amy laughed. "Her nose was all pointy?"

Susie tried to explain by telling us that when the tiny capillaries at the tip break down, the nose can get pointy. Her nursing instructor had told her this often happened when someone was dying.

Amy tried to rationalize the incident as well by proposing that Miss Z was beginning the dying process, and we had startled her when we touched her.

I'm not sure if we were too busy to continue thinking of explanations or if we settled on the ones already proposed, but we went about our morning, administering meds and proceeding with nursing care.

I was alone when I approached bed six again. It may have been anxiety, but I felt uncomfortable when I entered the room. Miss Z was sitting up. She was once again staring at the foot of the bed. She had terror in her eyes.

I called her name but she didn't respond. Her attention stayed fixed at the foot of her bed. She began breathing fast and heavy. "No, no, no, no, no, no," she kept saying.

I called her by name again.

She looked up at the ceiling pleadingly. "Please," she said and repeated it several times. She was reaching up to the ceiling with both arms.

I leaned over and grabbed the pole from which her IV line ran. One of its wheels was wedge between the base of her bed and the bottom of the small cabinet next to it. The tubing ran from the bag down to her arm. As she was reaching up, the tubing was getting taut and I was afraid the IV would be pulled out. Just as I freed the wheel and slid the pole closer to Miss Z, she dropped back onto the bed. Her head hit the pillow, and bobbed up and down.

"Please," she muttered. Her speech was fainter. She seemed exhausted.

It was time for me to bathe my patient. I retrieved her basin from the cabinet and went to the sink. Miss Z lay in bed, seemingly trying to catch her breath and relax. I set the basin on the over-bed tray. I loosened the ties on Miss Z's blue and white printed hospital gown and unfastened the snaps that were keeping the sleeve together so I could remove it without disturbing the IV line. I lifted off the gown and turned to place it in the bedside hamper.

My back was turned only for a second when I heard a bang. I turned to face Miss Z. She had sprung up from the bed again. This time, with such force she pushed the over-bed tray. The basin toppled over, spilling water over her, the bed and the floor.

I called her name again. "Are you okay?" My heart was pounding so hard, I could feel the pulsations in my ears.

She didn't acknowledge my words or presence. She was again fixated on the foot of her bed. "No," she screamed. The vowel dragged out. "No-o-o-o. Get out of here. Go away!"

I thought she might have been confused or hallucinating so I tried to reorient her. "You're in the hospital. I'm your nurse."

She ignored me.

I stared at her as I backed away. I was beginning to sweat.

Her face bore a look of terror, her eyes wide open and fixed on something I could not see. Her fists were clenched and she pulled her arms and legs into her body as though trying to protect herself. Then after a minute or two that seemed like hours, she dropped back down onto the bed.

I was expecting her to relax and try to catch her breath as she had done before but that didn't happen. Instead, she tightened her body. She extended her arms and clenched the rails on each side. She looked as though she was being pulled down into the mattress and was trying her best to fight it. She dug her heels in and her back and bottom lifted up.

I stepped back farther and looked outside to see where Susie and Amy were. Susie's white sneakers were visible underneath one of the curtains as she moved around another patient's bed. I called her name twice before I got her attention.

"What's up?" she asked, peeking out from the curtain that was protecting her patient's privacy.

I nodded toward Miss Z.

Susie disappeared behind the curtain for a few seconds, then reappeared heading toward me. "What's wrong?"

I didn't answer. I waved my hand toward Miss Z, who was writhing in the bed muttering the word *no* and phrases like *get out of here* and *leave me alone.* Her hands remained clenched on the side rails.

"I don't know what's happening," I told Susie. I told her about the water basin and she helped me. We dropped towels onto the floor and stooped to push them around and sop up the water. "This is freaking me out. Is it just me?"

"Something feels strange, all right," Susie assured me. "How long has this been going on?"

I explained what I had just witnessed. At first it was a few seconds of screaming followed by a period of time when Miss Z would begin to relax and rest for a while. But the current incident, or spasm, or whatever it was, had been going on for about ten minutes.

"Let's change the wet linens and get her into a dry gown." Susie sounded brave as she tugged on the soaked sheet.

Miss Z grabbed the sheet and Susie's hand. "Help me." She looked at Susie with pleading eyes.

Susie tried unsuccessfully to free her hand. "Ok. I am going to help you. Let go of my hand and let me get these wet sheets off you."

"*Help* me," she repeated maintaining her pleading stare and firm grip.

With Miss Z's attention focused on Susie, I was able to slip the wet sheet off. Then I worked to get the wet sheet out from under her. Susie continued to try to calm the patient and free herself. Neither worked, so I placed dry sheets on the bed while Miss Z was distracted.

"I don't think a bath is going to work here," I told Susie.

"Me neither. Maybe she doesn't need a bath right now."

Miss Z pulled Susie closer. "Don't let them take me. Please!"

"I won't but you have to let go of my hand."

I doubted Susie could really stop whomever it was that was supposedly taking this woman, but her assurance worked. Miss Z obeyed and dropped back onto the bed. Susie was free and the bed was now dressed in dry linens.

"Help me get the gown on before you go," I requested.

Susie walked over to me and whispered, "I'm going to get the Holy Water."

We kept a small clear plastic bottle with a black lid in one of the cabinets in our nurses' station. I'm not sure where it came from or who filled it, but it had *Holy Water* written on it in black letters. When I started in the ICU, the nurse who conducted my orientation explained that every once in a while, one of the priests would ask for it when he came to anoint a patient. No one had ever asked me for it before, but I knew where it was.

I left the room with Susie. "What are you going to do?" I asked.

"I don't know. Sprinkle it on her? Maybe whatever's trying to get her will go away."

The tiny hairs on my arms and legs and neck stood up. "Like an exorcism? Should we call a priest?"

Susie stood still, thinking over what I'd said. Then she walked briskly toward bed six with the plastic bottle gripped firmly in her hand.

"What if it burns her skin or causes welts like it does in the movies?" I was picturing Linda Blair's character, Regan, in *The Exorcist.* I had visions of Miss Z's head spinning around 360 degrees before she would spit some abnormal bile colored bodily fluid at us.

Susie opened the black cap on the bottle and sprinkled water over Miss Z. Nothing happened. No welts. No burns. She still writhed and moaned and pleaded.

Miss Z continued like this for hours. Each time I had to go to bed six to assess her or administer a medication, I felt nervous. Sometimes she was twisting her body and admonishing something. At other times, she was reaching for the ceiling and pleading for help.

"It's like *Poltergeist* over there," I said to Susie and Amy when we gathered in the nurses' lounge.

We missed our break and lunch was going to be a few bites of a sandwich eaten while sitting on the edge of our chairs so we could see the patients' cardiac monitors and hear the call bells. We had visiting hours at that time so some of the patients had company at their bedsides.

Miss Z was not one of them. No one came to visit or call to check on her. We could hear her screaming and pleading from anywhere in the unit. I washed my sandwich down with a gulp of iced tea and stood. "I better get back out there. The lab will be coming to draw blood work."

"Tell Satan I said hi," Amy said.

"Not funny. Tell you what, I'll work the desk and you can take Miss Z."

"No thanks!"

I checked on my other patients while I worked up the courage to head back to bed six. When I finally walked over to Miss Z, she was still twisting around with fists clenched. She was acting as if she was restrained by something and was trying to break free. I could see she was exhausted. Her heart rate was coming down and her breathing had slowed. But still, she kept fighting.

When the physician came to see her, he too was perplexed. He reviewed her chart and spoke with someone on the phone in our conference room. When he finally came out, I was at the bedside of another patient. He tapped on the window of the bay and motioned to me.

I finished up and joined him in the conference room. He told me he'd spoken with a colleague about Miss Z. She had no one listed as next of kin and since she had no living parents and no children, there was no one else with whom to consult. "I'm going to enact a DNR," he said.

This meant that if Miss Z were to die, we would not attempt to resuscitate her. There was nothing more we could do. The bleeding wasn't stopping and our efforts were futile.

"We'll just keep her comfortable," he said.

I nodded, rose from my chair, and left. I hoped the medications we would give to comfort her would stop the writhing and moaning.

There wasn't much left to my shift. I gave my report to the evening shift and told them I hoped their night with Miss Z would be more peaceful than my day.

I drove home but my mind stayed at work. I barely slept. It was strange. I'd slept all night after watching *The Exorcist* and after watching *Poltergeist*. Ghost stories and books about the supernatural had never bothered me. But somehow, being in a room with some unseen force disturbed me.

Sleep-deprived, I went to work the next day. I'd made up my mind to ask for a different assignment. But when I entered the ICU, Miss Z's bed was empty.

I went to the conference room, where one of the night shift nurses was waiting for us to gather for shift report. "What happened to bed six?" I asked her.

"She died."

"When?"

"Around two o'clock this morning."

"Was she at peace?"

The night shift nurse looked at me sympathetically and shook her head. "No. No, she wasn't."

* * *

I've never seen another dying this unsettling, before or since. As I've said, most of my patients seemed serene as death neared. As I watched them die, I would recall my own near-death experience. I remembered my time in the garden; the beautiful colors, the freedom from all stress and care. I liked to think that each dying man or woman was in his or her own garden, walking toward the light, feeling the euphoria. But I also wondered what Miss Z had seen that so terrified her.

I wished I could see what the dying saw. Or that I could interview them after they passed over. I think they may have the answers to all my questions.

I like a look of Agony,
Because I know it's true –
Men do not sham Convulsion,
Nor simulate, a Throe –

The eyes glaze once - and that is Death –
Impossible to feign
The Beads upon the Forehead
By homely Anguish strung.

–from "I Like A Look Of Agony" by Emily Dickinson

Six
IT'S SHOCKING:
When Resuscitation Works

When I completed school and became a registered nurse, I took a job at a small state-run hospital just down the street from my home. I worked the obligatory year on a medical-surgical unit and then transferred into the intensive care unit, or ICU.

To work in the ICU, I had to attend classes on how to read an electrocardiogram. I observed other nurses in emergency situations and attended training programs, such as the American Heart Association's Advanced Cardiac Life Support training, or ACLS. All this was to prepare me to take an active part in resuscitation efforts, or what we in health care refer to simply as "codes."

One day, a few hours into my shift, I had transferred my patient out of ICU and now had an empty bed among my assignments. It wasn't long before a nurse from the emergency department called.

"I'm calling with report on an admission we have for bed four," she said.

I took the report and got the room ready.

In most cases, getting an admission to the intensive care unit was something we would complain about because it usually involved a lengthy report and several pages of admission orders. When we got the call we were getting an admission, we moaned because we knew we would be tied up with work for at least two hours.

We would have to do a lengthy assessment of the new patient. I would have to start intravenous lines and hook the patient up to all of the equipment he or she would require: ventilator, urinary drainage catheter, nasogastric tube, and so on.

I would have to ask a list of questions about his or her health and medical history. In addition, since almost all the patients I admitted were elderly, they had long answers for every question and often did not understand or could not quite hear what it was I was asking.

"Were you ever in the hospital before?" I would ask.

"In a hostel?"

"No, a hospital."

"Oh, yes."

Then they would give me the details of each of the fifty-two hospitalizations they'd had over the past ninety years of life. I would then have to condense the story so it would fit on the three short lines provided on the admission form.

But this admission was different.

"Mr. G, patient of Dr. K, thirty-six, male. He's being admitted with an acute allergic reaction to bee stings," the emergency room nurse informed me. "We gave him epinephrine and Benadryl. Airway is patent. Vital signs are stable. No other history. He'll be up to you in a few minutes."

That's it? First of all, thirty-six was less than half the average age of all of our other patients. It was great to have a young guy for a change. He didn't require a complete bed bath. He didn't need to be suctioned. He had no dressings or tubes. There were no complicated procedures to perform. There were no orders other than to place him on the cardiac monitor and observe for complications. Cool, I thought, this one's going to be easy.

At the nurses' station, labeled boxes contained forms that would make up the patient's chart. (This was before digital records.) A form to record his vital signs. One for the physician to write orders. A form for me to record my observations. A form to post laboratory results. I pulled them from their boxes and organized them in the orange plastic binder that would be Mr. G's official medical record.

When the patient arrived, his sinewy body was leaning forward. No doubt he was anxious to get out of the wheelchair bringing him from the emergency department to the ICU. He was tanned from working outdoors, and his voice was husky as he joked with the orderly. It was rare to see an ICU admission laughing as he entered the strange world of beeps and buzzers.

"Hi, Mr. G." I walked alongside as the orderly maneuvered the wheelchair in. I introduced myself to my new patient and asked him to move out of the chair and onto the bed.

Mr. G stood. His hand was clasped firmly at the small of his back as he tried to keep the sides of his powder blue patient gown closed over his bare buttocks.

(No, I did not peek.)

He sat on the edge of the bed. "Spin around," I instructed. I patted the mattress up near the head to indicate that I needed him to rest his back against the mattress. Then I walked over to the other side and reached for the white, red and black wires I would attach to electrodes and place on Mr. G's chest.

The orderly pushed a button and raised the head of the bed until the mattress and Mr. G's back were aligned with each other. "Need anything else?" he asked both Mr. G and me. We both said no and thanked him. Then he took the wheelchair and left.

Mr. G realigned himself in the bed. "This okay?"

"You're fine." I smiled. I loosened the neck of the gown and attached three sticky electrodes in their proper position. The white electrode was secured just under his right clavicle, the black, just under his left clavicle. The red one was placed about six inches down from his armpit, near the apex of his heart.

"These pick up a signal from your heart," I told him. "It shows up on this monitor so we can see it." I pointed to the screen on the wall. Then, with the electrodes in place, I stared as a green line formed a pattern. I flipped a switch and a thin strip of paper flowed out of the monitor. I glanced at it, quickly counting the number of beats it recorded and making sure each had the necessary waveforms to indicate normal functioning of the heart. I placed the strip in my pocket, so I could secure it to the chart later on.

"How's it look?"

"Perfect. Normal sinus rhythm of eighty. You can't get any better than that."

I pushed the over-bed table close and opened the chart on top of it. I flipped through forms until I found the one I needed. "More questions," I warned with a chuckle.

"No problem."

I asked him to recount the events that had brought him to the ER that day and, subsequently, to the intensive care unit. I wrote in his chart as he provided me with the particulars. He had a side job cutting grass for his friend's landscaping business.

"The funny part about it all is that I cut the grass there every week, every summer. I hit a bees' nest there last summer and ended up in the hospital with an allergic reaction. I was in for two days. Now what are the chances the same thing would happen..."

He stopped. I looked up from my paperwork. Mr. G's eyes were open, staring blankly into space. His body had gone limp. I glanced up at the monitor, and gasped when I saw a green squiggly line. I recognized the rhythm as ventricular fibrillation or, in short, V-fib. I quickly slid my fingers into the groove of his neck. *No pulse!* He'd gone into cardiac arrest.

"Think V-fib, defib!" At one of my ACLS training programs, an instructor had told me that the sooner a person in ventricular fibrillation is shocked, or defibrillated, the better the chances are the rhythm will convert back to normal sinus rhythm. The words resounded in my head. *V-fib, defib. V-fib, defib.*

I lunged toward the crash cart and grabbed the paddles from their cradle. I charged them as I placed them on Mr. G's chest. I pushed the buttons and delivered two hundred joules of electricity. His body bounced up away from the mattress and then thumped back down.

I backed away from the patient and stood at his bedside clenching the defibrillator paddles in my sweaty palms, staring as I tried to regain my composure.

"...The same time last year." He scratched his chest in the two areas recently vacated by the defibrillator's paddles. "My chest is itchy."

He looked at me with one eyebrow raised then went back to telling me about the bees' nest.

I took a step back, amazed. Was this some sort of crazy prank? I expected to see the *Candid Camera* crew coming toward me at any moment. I'd had no idea it would be like this. I didn't expect to deliver the shock and have the patient finish his sentence.

When I'd learned about resuscitation, I'd hoped that when the time came I would know what to do. I prayed that if I had to defibrillate someone, it would work. But I never expected it to work so well that the patient wouldn't even realize that he had been dead for a moment.

I suddenly felt both powerful and powerless at the same time. Should I tell him he had just been dead? As he talked about the bees, I contemplated this. But somehow, saying *Excuse me, sir, but do you know you were just dead for a few seconds?* seemed inappropriate. So I decided to say nothing just then. Something told me to wait. There would be a better time to tell him what happened.

I picked up my pen and continued to write. When my shift was over, I went home satisfied. Wanting to save lives had been my reason for becoming a nurse. Actually being able to save one made all the training and tedious work worthwhile. This was one of those rare times I would see life triumph over death, and know I'd been instrumental in the victory.

* * *

I went on to become the instructor rather than the student at the ACLS training. As an instructor, I always taught my students to think "Vfib, defib" and I often shared this success story to give them hope.

We nurses see death so often it's easy to feel defeated by her. I didn't want the new nurses to give up. They could make a difference. They could save lives.

After three to four years, my students went out into the world to begin their own professional practice. Though many kept in touch, our story-swapping changed from classroom and clinical issues to engagements, weddings, breakups, children, and other personal events.

One morning, just around 5 A.M., my cell rang. I was startled awake by Cyndi Lauper singing "Girls just wanna have fun." I had set that song as my ring tone.

My first thought went to my three children, but they were all safe in the house. Next, they went to my extended family. Had something happened to my mother, or one of my sisters? I grabbed the phone and squinted at the screen. The name of a former student flashed across it. This particular student had graduated a few months before. Why was he calling me so early?

"Hello." My voice was still sleepy.

"Oh, man. Guess what! I just used the stuff you taught us in ACLS."

He was excited as he told me about the patient he'd just saved. He was proud as he announced his preceptor didn't have to coach him. He gave me blow by blow details. He knew what he was doing, and more importantly, it worked. He saved his patient. And although he was the one who did it, he was giving me a share in the credit.

I laughed and reminded him it was 5:00 A.M. But I thanked him for calling and letting me share his success. My former student would not always triumph over death. No health care professional does. But this had been such a victory, and I was grateful to have been instrumental in achieving it.

How odd the Girl's life looks
Behind this soft Eclipse -
I think that Earth feels so
To folks in Heaven – now –

– from "I'm 'Wife' – I've Finished That" by Emily Dickinson

Seven
MEMORIES AND MOTIVES:
How Experience Shaped a Career

W hat's the first word that comes to mind when I say *green*?

I'm sure you've played a similar game at some point. Someone says a word and then the next person in the group says the first word that occurs to them. I say *green* and the next in line says *tomato*. Then the next person plays off that to say *juice*. *Green*. *Tomato*. *Juice*. And so on.

Memories work the same way. I once saw a cow and remembered I had to buy a birthday present for my next-door neighbor's daughter. This association made complete sense to me because when I saw the cow, I thought of my daughter, Cornelia, who loves cows. That made me think of her best friend, Gina. Gina was our next-door neighbor, and she happened to be having a birthday the following week.

But there are other times when something triggers a memory or thought that seems to make no sense at all. As I began examining my attitudes toward death and dying, I had a lot of those moments. I would be doing something and suddenly have a thought that appeared to have no correlation at all to what I was doing. I wondered if I could somehow slow down the thought process and follow the path of a memory through my brain. Maybe if I could see how one thought led to another and another and another, death (or at least my attitudes about it) would make sense. Maybe if we could do that with our memories of people who have died, we could better understand our feelings about the process.

The idea of slowing my thought processes so I could see the associations came spontaneously one day. My son came in from school with the schedule for the high school marching band, in which he played trumpet.

"Mom," he said, handing me the schedule. "Do you think Nana and PapaGino will be able to come to the first football game to see me? I think we're playing at half time."

I didn't look at the schedule. I just continued preparing supper. "I don't know. Call them and tell them about it."

While he ran off to find one of the cordless phones (the ones that were never on the chargers where they belonged), I suddenly remembered that I needed to find a new EKG practice workbook for a class I would be teaching in the spring semester at Wilkes University.

I stopped what I was doing, found a pen and jotted a quick note to myself. But when I returned to meal preparation, I found myself wondering how I'd gotten from the band schedule to a workbook on electrocardiograms. That's when I decided to try to slow down my memory associations and see what would happen.

I thought about my thirteen-year old son posing for pictures in his green, gold and white band uniform. He was standing in front of a tree on our lawn holding his trumpet. The breeze was swaying the tall feather on his band cap.

"Smile," I instructed.

He rolled his eyes and smirked.

The next thing I knew, I was reliving a memory about him when he was three. It was 1996. He was out in our backyard with my father. His face was serious as he watched my father pierce the weed-infested grass with his shovel.

As usual at that time in his life, my son was dressed in his excavation outfit. His denim shirt was tucked neatly into his khaki shorts with a plastic tool belt fastened around his thin waist. He wore his favorite shoes: a pair of tan Buster Brown hardhat-style boots. Ever since my parents had bought him a book about *Jurassic Park*, he seemed intent on being a paleontologist, though the word itself was bigger than he was.

My father was digging a hole and my son was kneeling at his feet. His big blue eyes took in every move my father made. I could practically see the mental notes he was making. I peered through the railing of the deck and watched as they worked diligently on their latest project.

As they dug deeper into the ground in my memory, I began digging deeper inside my mind. It was as though I were shoveling through my past. I burrowed through memories until I reached my own childhood.

Images flashed. I was a young woman, watching my father hold my newborn son for the first time. I was seeing my father's face after he walked me down the aisle on my wedding day. I was a teenager backing my father's red Honda Civic over a curb as he tried to teach me to drive a stick shift. I was a young girl listening patiently in his boat as he tried to teach me to bait a hook. I was a little girl holding my father's hand as he took me to the comic book store, where he would buy me the latest issue of *Hot Stuff* or *Archies*. I was a child going with my father to visit his parents on a Sunday afternoon. I was six, standing in the archway of the kitchen at my grandparent's house.

* * *

It was 1970. Grampy was sitting at the old maple table in the kitchen of the company home where he and my grandmother lived. From my six-year old perspective, things didn't seem right. The room wasn't filled with the aroma of carrots and tomatoes from Gram's stew and it seemed odd Grampy didn't have his big white enamel pot filled with water. He should have been all ready to cut an orange into wedges. Then my sister and I could eat the juicy fruit and put the rinds in the water. And Grampy could make origami boats that would sail on the rinds.

"I want to make orange peel soup." I stood with my hands on my hips.

"Go watch television with your sister," my mother ordered. She sounded upset.

None of the grownups turned toward me. They were all huddled around the table with serious faces.

I wondered what was wrong with my parents and my gram and my aunt and uncle. Why were they so somber? Gram's house was always filled with laughter. Why wasn't anyone laughing?

"I want to make orange peel soup." I repeated, hoping my grandfather would indulge me. When he didn't, I stomped away and threw myself onto the oversized avocado recliner in the adjacent room.

My older sister sat quietly on the couch watching the television. Images of black, white and gray moved around the screen but I didn't register anything. I was more interested in what was going on in the kitchen. That was until a weird car came around the corner. Its sirens were louder than the television and its lights were much more colorful.

I jumped to my feet and raced to the front door. The car looked like the 1960s Batmobile. But it was white and had the word *ambulance* on the side. Red lights were spinning on its roof. The excitement of its arrival distracted me from the activities in the kitchen. I watched through the screen as it parked in front of the house and two men got out. They had some sort of cart with them and were carrying boxes that looked like the kind my dad took with him when we went fishing. One of the grownups let them in and my sister and I took advantage of their arrival and followed them into the kitchen.

No one seemed to notice me standing by the table watching the men as they worked. I heard my father tell one of the men that Grampy worked in the mines. I liked hearing his mining stories and wished he would tell me one now. But he didn't tell any stories to either me or to the two men.

While my sister crouched in the corner next to the large white stove, I watched curiously as one man put a mask on Grampy's face and connected it with a long tube to a grayish green tank that looked like a giant bullet. My sister and some of the grownups were crying. It didn't cross my mind to wonder why. There were too many exciting things happening. I'd never seen anything like it, not even when I had snuck into the family room when my parents thought I was asleep and watched *Medical Center* or *Marcus Welby, MD* on the television. Though some of the things these two men had reminded me of those shows.

The pair helped Grampy onto the cart, rolled him out through the front door, and slid him into the back of the Batmobile.

"Where are they taking Grampy?"

"To the hospital."

"Why?" I asked again and again over the next few days. "When can I see him?"

It seemed they never answered my questions to my liking. So I just asked over and over and hoped for a more pleasing answer.

My parents tried to explain that children weren't allowed in hospitals. They told me something about germs that could make me sick. I didn't care about the germs. I just wanted to see Grampy.

But a visit to see my grandfather was not on the agenda. Instead, I spent my days in the first grade and my evenings doing homework. It was early December and, with Christmas just a few weeks away, we were busy with preparations at the school.

I went each day, bundled in the green and white plaid winter coat and matching Kelly green scarf my grandmother had made me. I returned each day, clumsily carrying the project du jour in my mittens. I was always cold, so I looked forward to getting to the warm house. I didn't know what it was, but on that particular day, that warmth didn't take away the chill. Instead, I felt goose bumps popping up all over my arms. I looked around the living room trying to figure out what was happening.

"Grampy died," someone explained.

I can't remember who delivered the news or how exactly they told me this. I just remember that it didn't make sense. I didn't really know what the word "died" meant. It seems uncharacteristic now, but for some reason, I didn't even ask for an explanation.

A day or two later one of my parents told me they were taking me to see Grampy. I thought perhaps they'd changed the rules of the hospital or that suddenly no one cared about hospital germs. It didn't matter. The only words I could hear in my head were "You can go to see Grampy tonight." Those words made me happy. Of course, at that age, I didn't realize that seeing him didn't mean he was going to be like I expected. At six, I thought he would be sitting up with his white enamel pot in front of him. And that we would make boats out of paper and float them on orange peels.

When it was time for my visit, we didn't go to the hospital, nor did we go to Grampy's. Instead my mother and father took me to a new house. The new house smelled like a combination of incense, roses, breath mints and perfume. They led me through a big foyer and down a long hallway. Then I saw Grampy. He was sleeping in some big box with red roses on top of it.

I ran up to him. "Grampy!"

He didn't answer.

"Is he going to wake up?" I looked up toward the grownups.

My mother dabbed tears. "Just give him a little kiss," she instructed.

I climbed up on the step in front of the box. Standing on my tippy-toes, I stretched toward Grampy and touched my lips to his cheek.

"Yuck! He feels like salami!" I turned to my parents and pouted.

My parents took me into a different room. It was just the three of us. They told me God took Grampy to live with him in Heaven. I didn't get it but they offered no other explanation, so I just nodded. Maybe it would make sense another day.

But days and weeks and months passed and it still didn't make sense. I missed him terribly. But I had a plan.

My mother had once told me that whenever I went to a new church, I could make a wish. It seemed fool-proof. They did, after all, tell me that it was God who'd taken Grampy from us. So, why not just go to His house and make a wish? It made complete sense. I simply went into new churches and asked God to give my grandfather back. It never happened. He never came back.

He wasn't there when I finished elementary school and moved on to high school. He wasn't there to take my side when I became a teenager and argued over curfew with my parents. As I plowed forward through my memories, it occurred to me that he wasn't there for anything. He wasn't there when I graduated from high school. Nor when I had graduated from nursing school. I wondered if there were any way he could even know that I had become a nurse or that I once worked at the hospital where he died.

* * *

My memory association took me to 1987. I'd been a nurse for two years and had been working in the critical care unit for less than one.

It was Easter time, so my parent's house smelled like hyacinths and baked ham. I walked down the steps to the family room. My dad was lying on the sofa with the lights off. When I flicked on the switch, his skin was a milky shade of pale gray. He was sweating.

"Dad? What are you doing?"

He didn't open his eyes. "My jaw hurts. Just leave me rest here awhile."

I was new to critical care, but I'd had enough education and experience (and years of CPR training) to know he needed medical attention. The pain associated with a heart attack wasn't always in the chest. It could manifest in the back, the shoulder, the neck, or the jaw. And one of the first things we were taught was that *the highest incidence of death from cardiac arrest after the onset of the pain was in the first hour.* I had no idea how long he had been lying there on the couch. I had to act quickly.

The hospital was just down the street, so within minutes my family was huddled inside the ER waiting room. It felt peculiar to be sitting in the waiting room of the hospital where I worked. I didn't like being on the family's side of things.

The emergency room physician came out and called me by name. He handed me the printout of my father's electrocardiogram. I looked at it systematically, as I'd been taught. There were changes in the ST segments in leads II, III and avF. Even with my limited experience, I knew part of my father's heart wasn't getting enough blood. Without immediate attention, he would end up having a heart attack or, even worse, a cardiac arrest.

"He's lucky you made him come." The doctor patted my shoulder. Then he explained to us that they would be transferring my father to a larger hospital just a few miles away.

His hospital stay seemed like a blur. I tried to stop being a nurse and to assume the role of daughter. I didn't want to look at lab values and follow-up EKGs. I didn't want to hear about medications that were being prescribed or treatments that were being done. I wanted to sit down and have someone tell me everything was going to be okay.

In a few days, my father was discharged and I was being congratulated by the cardiologists and nurses for my actions. I didn't care about the praise. I was just thankful that he was alive and still with me.

That memory returned me to the present, where my dad and son played in my backyard. My son squealed as he worked at his imaginary excavation site.

"Ah Greer!" My son yelled out his version of "all clear."

The hole was dug and my father had rigged up some contraption with wood and rope.

My son adjusted his yellow hard hat and yelled again. "Ah Greer!"

My father yanked the rope and dirt was catapulted into the air like brown fireworks. My son jumped up and down, clapping and screaming. "Again, Pa Gino! Again!"

My seemingly disparate memory associations suddenly made sense. They were linked to my reasons for becoming a nurse, more specifically, a cardiac nurse. I wanted to save lives, I reminded myself. But I wondered if perhaps it wasn't really *lives* I wanted to save, but *one* life: a life that would give my son multitudes of moments with his grandfather rather than just the few isolated memories I have of mine.

The grief over my grandfather's death ignited a passion in me. And although it had been an unconscious passion, it propelled me to make a difference. There was nothing I could do to change the past, but as a nurse, there was plenty I could do to affect the future. I was determined to gain some sort of control over death.

O powerful western fallen star!

O shades of night—O moody, tearful night!

O great star disappear'd—O the black murk that hides the star!

O cruel hands that hold me powerless—O helpless soul of me!

O harsh surrounding cloud that will not free my soul.

– from "When Lilacs Last in the Dooryard Bloom'd" by Walt Whitman

Eight
REARRANGING THE DECK CHAIRS:
The Burden and Benefit of Treatment

In the fall of 1994, NBC debuted the hospital drama *ER*. In the early episodes, John Carter (played by Noah Wyle) was a medical student, eager to save the world. In episode eleven of season two, Carter was assigned to a patient named Mrs. Rubadoux. Mrs. Rubadoux had a ruptured aortic aneurysm that had been repaired in surgery. Due to pre-existing conditions, after the surgery her heart was failing. In other words, it couldn't pump a sufficient volume of blood to the rest of her body and she was failing.

In health care, practitioners constantly have to weigh burden against benefit when making decisions about providing care. Medications have contraindications, meaning you can't use them in patients with specific conditions. For instance, you can't give specific medications to patients with certain allergies or with damage to their kidneys. And they have side effects. A medication is given to have a desired effect, but it can also have undesired effects. At times, the undesired effects can be so detrimental, they outweigh the benefits the desired effects can have. And this was the case with Mrs. Rubadoux.

Her blood pressure was dropping. Carter went through all the possible meds he could use to help her. Each was either contraindicated in her case or it had side effects that would make her worse. Carter spent his entire day titrating medications and adjusting treatments to keep his patient alive.

Toward the end of the episode, he discussed Mrs. Rubadoux's condition with the chief of surgery, Dr. Carl Vucelich, played by actor Ron Rifkin. Carter was trying to find a way to keep her alive and was pitching ideas for treatment options.

Dr. Vucelich scoffed. "She's a sinking ship, and you're rearranging her deck chairs." He then added, "She's dying, Mr. Carter. Nothing you do is going to change that."

That scene always stuck with me. As a nurse, I found myself in similar situations all the time. Weighing benefits and burdens of care. Making an effort even when I knew nothing I did would change the outcome. Then again, sometimes, our efforts aren't about saving the dying, but rather about granting the survivors a sense of contentment.

That particular *ER* episode aired in 1996. Seven years later, I found myself weighing benefits and burdens in my personal life.

* * *

My father came home from a hockey game complaining of back pain. When it didn't ease with rest and medication, he decided it was time to visit his primary doctor. He had a history of muscle spasms in his back, but in the past the pain had gone away after he took a muscle relaxant or a few doses of analgesics. His doctor didn't know why this time it was different, so he began ordering consults and tests.

With every consult and diagnostic study, we waited to hear a diagnosis and prognosis. After a few weeks of testing, an MRI found a large mass near the spinal cord in his lower back. We moved into further studies and a biopsy to figure out what the mass was. Was it a tumor on the spinal cord itself? In the abdominal cavity? Bone? Lymph nodes? Once again we waited for a diagnosis and prognosis. And as a health care provider, I found myself trying to get as much information as possible. I wanted to know if he was a sinking ship or not. I promised myself that I wouldn't be naïve and insist we keep rearranging the deck chairs if there was no hope of staying afloat.

Finally, the results of the biopsy came back and he was diagnosed with B cell non-Hodgkins lymphoma. After the initial shock, we were told the prognosis was good. There were chemotherapeutic agents that could kill these specific cancerous cells. We were all in good spirits after this news. My son even joked that if his grandfather lost his hair after chemo, he would shave his head so they would look like twins. Yes, we were in luck. We were told he wouldn't even lose his hair; the chemo for this type of lymphoma had few side effects.

As months and years went by, he fought his cancer. He went to the clinic for chemotherapy every few months. And if you saw him, you would never know anything was wrong. He still had his sense of humor and everyone who cared for him got to know him and admired how he faced cancer with a positive attitude. He was always in a good mood and was never self-pitying.

After a series of treatments, he had another MRI. The tumor was shrinking. The benefit of the chemotherapy outweighed the burden. More treatments and another MRI and the tumor got even smaller. Finally, after even more treatments and another MRI, the oncologist gave us good news. My father was finally cancer free!

A few months later, he talked about getting more chemo. I didn't understand. "If you no longer have cancer, why are you still getting chemotherapy?" He explained it to me the way his oncologist had explained it to him. He would get chemo to prevent the cancer from coming back.

I didn't like this. Why not continue to do scans and if it were to recur, he could start chemo again then?

Although we'd been told the drug had minimal side effects, chemotherapy wiped him out. It made him tired. It made him prone to infections. But he was a compliant patient and believed his oncologist knew best. So every few months, he went to the clinic. The entire time, I argued with him. I didn't see how this could benefit him more than it would burden him. He was just beginning to rebuild his immunity and with each treatment, it would be wiped out again.

Ten years after his initial diagnosis of B-cell non-Hodgkins lymphoma, he was in remission but still receiving chemo. He said he felt good, but it didn't seem to be true. He lost weight. He complained about weakness in his legs. And he was not one to complain—ever! He fell a few times. Although he kept saying he was okay, everyone was concerned. My mother insisted he go to his primary physician again to get checked.

The doctor advised my dad to discuss his symptoms with the oncologist. But the specialist told him they had nothing to do with either lymphoma or the continuing chemo. After several more appointments with his primary doctor, and a series of other consults, we were getting nowhere. Orthopedic specialists, neurologists, urologists, no one could explain what was happening.

I was in my final semester of my graduate nursing program and teaching at a university. I had time off from my job for spring break but had a lot of work to do to finish my Masters degree. I planned on devoting all week to my thesis. Punxsutawney Phil had predicted six more weeks of winter so it was cold and damp outside and there was nothing to distract me. But on the very first day of break, at five in the morning, my mother called, near hysteria. My father was lying in bed and couldn't move.

Somehow my older sister and I got together and rushed to our parents' house. We arrived just as the ambulance did. My father told the ambulance crew he had to go to the bathroom but was unable to get up and ended up wetting himself. I stood back. Part of me was being a daughter and trying to stay out of the way of the EMTs and paramedics and the rest of me was being a nurse, using my clinical judgment skills and trying to figure out what was going on.

The crew loaded my father into the ambulance and my sister, my mother and I followed in our car. My head was running through a thousand scenarios of diagnoses and prognoses. I can't even recall who drove to the ER or anything else about the trip there.

At some point, we were settled in a bay. The room was dimly lit and the emergency room seemed quiet as nurses and doctors and other health care workers prepared for the shift change from night shift staff to day shift. After a bit of a wait, there was a steady stream of nurses and technicians asking my father questions. I noticed he was not articulating clearly. Everything sounded garbled. I pointed this out but my concern was dismissed and my mother blamed it on dehydration. I didn't agree, but I was having a hard time getting anyone from the health care team to hear me out. They'd made their assessments and moved on to other tasks. As my family waited in the dimly lit room, the emergency department on the other side of the bay was stirring with activity.

After several hours, a physician's assistant came in and told us my father had had a stroke. It wasn't a traditional stroke like you would read about in American Heart Association pamphlets. It wasn't in the artery that supplies the part of the upper brain that controls one side of the body. So he didn't have facial drooping or weakness in one arm or leg. Instead, the stroke had occurred in the brain stem.

As a nurse, I knew the cranial nerves that control the facial muscles come off the brain stem. We use those facial muscles to articulate sounds like pah-pah-pah, gah-gah-gah and lah-lah-lah. So the diagnosis seemed to make sense. The physician's assistant showed us the scan and pointed out small white patches distributed throughout the brain stem. Now things didn't make sense again. White patches? Diffuse distribution? That didn't sound like a stroke to me, but I needed time to process.

They admitted my dad to the neurological unit and consulted a neurologist. It was not the neurologist he had seen in the past and we all thought a new opinion might have been a good thing. Once he was settled in, my sister and I left our mom with him and went back to our homes to check on our families and get ourselves organized for the rest of the day.

I found myself not content with the diagnosis given to us by the physician's assistant. So I did what any nurse would do: I started searching the medical journal database.

I typed *brain stem* and *diffuse white patches*. The chemotherapy agent my father had been getting came up in several of the articles. According to the journals, long-term use of this particular agent could cause a condition known as progressive multifocal leukoencephalopathy or PML. That made sense. When immunity is compromised, as it is with long-term chemo, the body's ability to fight infections is lowered and viruses can enter any organ, including the brain. PML is characterized by diffuse white patches in the brain stem. As the name suggests, the condition is progressive. According to the articles, prognosis was poor and survival was six months at best.

I felt sick. I didn't want to believe it, so I didn't. But when the neurologist came on his consult, I made certain I was present and I mentioned the chemo and asked about PML. He seemed dismissive but did agree to perform a spinal tap to test for the JC virus—one known to cause PML in patients with compromised immunity. The tap was performed but we never got the results. My father was discharged without a diagnosis. After several phone calls to the neurologist, I was told the spinal tap was negative but was not able to get a diagnosis.

I was angry. My father showed no improvement, he had no diagnosis, and nothing was being done about his speech and weakness. After several calls to his primary doctor, he was referred to another neurologist in a town farther from home.

My mother and I went with him on the visit. I watched as the neurologist performed a thorough exam. My dad had no gag reflex and not one cranial nerve—there are twelve—was functioning properly. The new neurologist scheduled him for swallowing studies and referred him to a speech and language pathologist.

It was Easter time. On Good Friday, just a day after his swallowing studies, and before the speech and language pathologist was scheduled to come to his home, my mother received a phone call from the neurologist. My father had failed the swallowing studies. With no gag reflex and poor muscle tone, he was at risk for aspiration. If he tried to swallow food, the epiglottis might not cover his airway and food would go down into his lungs, or he could choke and completely block his airway. The neurologist told her not to let my father eat anything and to take him to the hospital immediately.

My family and my two sisters and their families were all gathered at my parents' home. We planned on dinner together. My sisters and I were anxiously waiting to hear what the phone call was about. Food was not on our minds. My father, on the other hand, was shoveling macaroni and cheese into his mouth the entire time my mother was on the phone receiving the test results and instructions. She waved her arms at him and tried to mime to us that he was to stop eating. In the chaos, our communication was not effective.

My mother hung up and we all got in our cars and drove nearly an hour to the hospital. Dad was admitted and a feeding tube was inserted through his nose and down into his stomach.

When I finally got back that night, it was late, but I couldn't sleep. I reread the articles about PML. It seemed too coincidental. He'd received long-term chemotherapy. His immune system was compromised. It was that time of year when everyone seemed to have some sort of virus. And all of the signs and symptoms were exactly the same as in the article. Was my father a sinking ship? Were we simply rearranging deck chairs? I hoped not.

On Easter Monday, I was off from school for the last day of holiday break, so I went to the hospital and spent the day with my father and my mother, who refused to leave her husband's side. A different neurologist was covering for the one he'd seen a few days prior. The new neurologist introduced himself and asked questions to clarify the events leading to my father's admission.

Since I had the doctor's ear, I mentioned PML. He agreed that my father's signs and symptoms did seem typical of PML and that the long-term administration of chemotherapy would make him susceptible. He would pull my father's records from his previous hospitalization so he could look at the test results. A few days later, they repeated the tests. In the meantime, the muscles in my father's face and neck had become so weak, he was having problems swallowing. He aspirated. In other words, food that should have been pushed down into the stomach when he swallowed was instead pushed into his lungs. He was moved to a critical care unit and a feeding tube was inserted through his abdomen, directly into his stomach.

We spent the next couple of days driving back and forth to the hospital. We were all trying to balance caring for our children and working with keeping abreast of my father's care.

I'd just come home from work when my mother called. The case manager at the hospital wanted us to come in for a family meeting to plan my father's care.

The hour-long drive was quiet. Our only conversations were short ones with long periods of silence in between. One of us would make a prediction about what the plan of care would entail and the others would shrug. None of us knew what to expect.

We were able to visit with my dad for a while. Then we were led into a conference room. I stared at the wood grain patterned table as nurses, nursing and medical students, and case managers trickled in. One of them was from the school where I taught. She'd been assigned to my father as part of her clinical experience. I felt comforted at seeing a familiar face. She was a good student, so I knew my dad was getting good care. But I also felt vulnerable. A student was seeing me, not as a confident and knowledgeable instructor and professional, but as a helpless, scared daughter.

Once all parties were seated, one of the women began. Two sentences into her monologue, she mentioned hospice. I was still trying to process. I'm not sure if I was in denial or depression but I didn't move. My sister and mother, on the other hand, were clearly in the anger phase. My mother was saying something about them not even trying and my sister was yelling that we weren't going to give up on my dad. We didn't even have a diagnosis, yet we were expected to make a decision. They didn't want to hear anything about hospice at this point. The meeting ended quickly with no plan made.

Later that day, the neurologist sat with my older sister and me in a quiet hallway. He confirmed the diagnosis of PML. I appreciated that he was honest and up front about the diagnosis and prognosis. He was kind and compassionate, but all I kept hearing as he discussed our options was *ER's* Dr. Vucelich. "A sinking ship" . . . "rearranging . . . deck chairs" . . . "dying" . . . "Nothing you do is going to change that."

In the days that followed, my father was transferred to a facility closer to home. He was placed in a progressive care unit while my mother was allowed time to adjust to the diagnosis. I would visit with him and then at night, I would lie in my bed and go through every detail of his treatment from his initial diagnosis of B-cell non-Hodgkins lymphoma to the chemo in remission. Should I have insisted the treatments stop? Should I have looked up the complications then instead of waiting until it was too late?

Finally, my father was moved to hospice, where he died—a long seven years after the start of his chemo and a mere two months after the symptoms of PML began.

Years have passed since. At night, when I'm alone, I find myself reliving each day since the onset of my father's back pain. I hear the words spoken to Mr. Carter over and over.

Perhaps if I had placed the deck chairs in a chevron pattern . . .

Where has fail'd a perfect return, indifferent of lies or the truth?

Is it upon the ground, or in water or fire? or in the spirit of man?

or in the meat and blood?

– from "All Is Truth" by Walt Whitman

Nine
HONESTY IS SUCH A LONELY WORD:
Who Talks to the Survivors?

After four years as a registered nurse at a small state hospital in my hometown, I thought I should move on to something bigger. I had a lot of experience yet wanted even more. So I took a job in the city of Wilkes-Barre.

What I didn't realize about being in a larger hospital was that I didn't quite have the breadth of experience I'd thought I had. I was no longer the big fish in the small pond. I was now more like a goldfish in the ocean. But I refused to let it get to me.

One incident comes to mind when I think about that transition. It happened shortly after I'd completed my three-month probation in a step-down unit. Although I'd been involved in resuscitations, or codes, in my past job, in my new one I wasn't assigned to the code team. Somehow, even though I realized that this facility was unlike the one I had come from, I didn't quite expect it to be so dissimilar.

* * *

I was working the 3-11 p.m. shift. After receiving the report from the nurses on the previous shift, we each went out to our assigned patients. I went to each of mine and introduced myself. Then I checked each patient's vital signs, assessed them and asked if they needed anything. Finished, I went back to the station to record my findings in the charts.

"Excuse me!" A woman in her late thirties placed manicured hands on the counter. Her perky voice interrupted the idle chitchat of the nurses gathered there. "We're going to go get something to eat. Our father's supper tray came, so we may as well go to the cafeteria while he eats," she said with a smile. "He was wondering if he could get some Mylanta. Guess he has an upset stomach."

"If it's not upset now, wait until after he eats the hospital food," one of the nurses joked. It was a common joke we used with families and we'd gotten to know Mr. Healey's son and daughter well enough over the last two days since his admission to know they would appreciate the humor without taking offense.

When Mr. Healey was admitted with chest pain, all tests had indicated it wasn't related to his heart. He was to stay a day or two longer while tests were run to look for other possible causes. His stomach was one of the things that would need to be evaluated, so the request for Mylanta didn't seem odd. Pain from gastric reflux was often confused with chest pain. Once a heart attack was ruled out, Mylanta was a standard order.

I went into the medication room and poured a dose of Mylanta into a clear plastic medicine cup. "Enjoy your dinner," I yelled down the hallway to Mr. Healey's daughter and son. Despite what most people think, hospitals are rarely quiet and nurses rarely whisper.

Mr. Healey's son and daughter smiled. The thinness of their lips and the way they curved over their small teeth made them look like their father. They waved before vanishing into the elevator.

"Be right back," I told my coworkers at the desk, who were writing up their charts. We too had hopes of grabbing supper before the second half of our 3-11 p.m. shift. I was hungry, so I hurried down to the last room on the left to give Mr. Healey his antacid.

I entered the room already talking. "Here's your aperitif," I started to joke.

But something was terribly wrong. The skin on my patient's face, which had been a rosy shade of pink since admission, was as white and chalky as the medication in my hand.

I quickly placed the cup of milky fluid on the over-bed table next to his untouched dinner and placed my hands on Mr. Healey's shoulders. "Are you okay?" I shook him.

There was no response. I ran to the door and jutted my head out. "Someone get the crash cart!" Then I dashed back into the room. Grabbing the corners of the over-bed table, I pushed it aside and impatiently jabbed the button that lowered the head of his bed.

"Code A. Sixth Floor. Code A. Sixth floor." The announcement came over the PA in a soft voice.

Although this was the proper way to announce a cardiac arrest to the staff, the nonchalant tone irritated me. "Hurry up," I yelled, aiming my words at the silver toned speaker in the ceiling. I missed being in the ICU at the state hospital. I knew where everything was there. I didn't need to wait for a code team to arrive.

"Holy crap," one of the other nurses muttered as she bolted in with the bulky red metal crash cart. She steered it close to Mr. Healey's head and left shoulder.

"Thank you!" I blurted. It had probably been less than a minute since I'd activated the alarm, but it seemed like forever.

I pulled the sheets off Mr. Healey's body and ripped off his gown. His abdomen and chest were a dusky shade of purplish gray. I ran my fingers across his chest and found my hand placement on the lower half of his breastbone. I began chest compressions.

A respiratory technician hurried in. "He's blue. What happened?"

"I - don't - know," I replied with each word spoken separately as to not interrupt the rhythm of the compressions. "I - found – him - slumped – over – when – I – walked – in."

Within minutes, the code team arrived. This consisted of the emergency room physician and two registered nurses trained in the principles and techniques of Advanced Cardiac Life Support, or ACLS. They spent hours each year learning, reviewing, and practicing what they needed to know in moments like this. And they knew it so well, that when they responded to a code, their actions seemed reflexive.

I watched enviously as they pushed their way around in the crowded room until each was in the position he or she had been trained to assume. The respiratory therapist stood behind the head of the bed. He had removed the headboard and was providing oxygen with a bag that looked like a blue football with a mask attached. The physician was at Mr. Healey's right side, next to me. His hands were tucked into the pockets of his lab coat.

A tall blond nurse from the cardiac care unit pushed past my coworker and took her position in front of the crash cart. She wore powder blue scrubs and had a purple stethoscope draped around her neck. She opened the top drawer of the cart and ran her fingers over the rows of prepackaged medications. A matronly-looking nurse from the emergency department stood at the foot of the bed. She propped the clipboard that held the resuscitation record against her hip. She had a roll of tape and a pair of bandage scissors tied to the drawstring of her cranberry scrub pants.

I wished I could have been part of the team. I knew what to do. I'd done it in my previous job. But they moved around as though I didn't exist.

My coworker began spouting a report to Dr. M. "This is Mr. Healey. Sixty-eight year old male admitted through the ER two days ago with complaints of...."

Dr. M shook his head. He removed one hand from the pocket of his crisp white lab coat and traced the curve of his well-groomed black mustache with his thumb. Then he extended his arm and waved it stiffly over the bed, stopping my coworker's words and my CPR. He ran his index finger across Mr. Healey's chest. "See this line?"

We all stared at a distinct line. Above it, the skin was pale and chalky, with a grayish cast. Below the line, the skin was purple and mottled.

"He ruptured a ventricular aneurysm," Dr. M shook his head again and sighed. "There's nothing we can do." His expression never changed. If he were frustrated, he didn't show it. No smile, no grimace. I imagined he would be good at poker, but he hardly seemed like the type of guy who would play. He glanced at the shiny gold Rolex watch on his wrist. "Time of death, eighteen fifty two."

I stepped away from the bed, my eyes still fixated on the line on Mr. Healey's chest. I wanted to speak, but I didn't. *Can't we keep trying? He was just talking a few minutes ago. His family said so. How did this all happen so fast?*

I took a deep breath and exhaled forcefully as I tried to push out every last ounce of adrenaline inside me. My spirits drooped with my shoulders. Ventricular aneurysm? I'd never even heard of such a thing. I stared at the line and made a mental note, just in case I should see this again. I felt depressed. I don't know if it was because I didn't get to do anything at the code or because I felt naïve for not knowing about a ventricular aneurysm.

Reluctantly, I took a pen from the pocket of my cranberry scrubs, scribbled 6:52 p.m. on a piece of paper and then slid the sheet and pen back into my pocket.

As the code team shuffled out, my coworker patted my arm. "I'll take the IV out. Why don't you get a basin with some soapy water and we'll wash him up." She pointed to patches of conductive gel that remained on Mr. Healey's chest after she peeled off the electrodes the CCU nurse had applied.

I was relieved I wouldn't have to be alone in the room with the body. Not that I was afraid. I just preferred that someone else be there with me. So, I accepted her offer with a nod before I plodded down the hallway. Just a few feet ahead, I saw Dr. M's perfect posture as he strolled toward the elevator. I was just a bit past the nurses' station when I saw Mr. Healey's daughter and son returning to the unit.

"Doctor!" I shouted to his back as the family approached.

The physician hit the elevator button and glanced back. "Yes?"

"These are Mr. Healey's children." I pointed.

He gave them a nod and stepped into the elevator. Holding the door with his hand, he leaned out. "Bring me the death certificate when you get a chance." His voice was as monotone as it had been at Mr. Healey's bedside.

"Death certificate?" The two grown children asked at the same time.

I glanced at the closed elevator doors in disbelief. Why was he doing this to me? I'd never told a family their loved one had died. At my former job, the doctors always did that. I was angry with Dr. M and nervous about the news I had to deliver to these kind people I had just met. What am I going to say? What am I *supposed* to say?

Before speaking, I reminded myself I had taken this new job to get more experience. I reviewed the rules I had learned. *State the death as fact. Keep it simple. Stay calm. Don't cry.* I swallowed hard and took a deep breath. Then I turned back to Mr. Healey's family and waved toward a small conference room. "Why don't the two of you join me in here?"

* * *

Whether telling someone his or her loved one has died, or hearing the news of my own loved one's death, it never gets easier. I know how to present myself. I know what I'm supposed to say. I know what I'm supposed to do. But I will never get over having to do it.

Then with the knowledge of death as walking one side of me,

And the thought of death close-walking the other side of me,

And I in the middle as with companions, and as holding the hands of companions,

I fled forth to the hiding receiving night that talks not,

Down to the shores of the water, the path by the swamp in the dimness,

To the solemn shadowy cedars and ghostly pines so still.

– from "When Lilacs Last in the Dooryard Bloom'd" by Walt Whitman

Ten
THE WAITING IS THE HARDEST PART:
The Dying Can Wait

IT was routine to admit patients to an Intensive Care
Unit who had conditions with high mortality rates.
They were not terminal, because there was still a chance
for recovery, no matter how slim. But sometimes,
treatments did not work or treatments had complications,
and the patients' conditions actually worsened after
admission. The doctors and nurses were then faced with
explaining to the patients' significant others that there was
really no more that they could do.

Hospice care was an option many families choose for
their loved ones. Other families held on to hope and prayed
for a miracle. And so, the patient remained in the ICU until
they died.

Over the years, caring for the dying had become familiar
for me. But as I learned through these experiences, death could
be unfair. For instance, one man abandoned his wife and
children to engage in a high-risk lifestyle. But death spared
him, and allowed him to continue his self-indulgent way of
life. Another selflessly and consistently put his wife and
children before himself. Yet death took him from them with
little or no warning.

Another injustice I've seen over and over, unfortunately,
is the sudden, unexpected death of a child. I can't imagine

how a mother must feel when she gets news her son or daughter was killed in a motor vehicle accident. She must bury her child without ever having the chance to speak to him or her again.

There were other times when death *was* fair. When She allowed a person to die on his or her own terms, for example. I can recall many instances in which human beings were allowed to cling to life until someone told them it was okay to go. This permission sometimes needed to come from a specific person. I recall one patient who needed her future son-in-law to promise he would take care of her daughter. At other times it may have been a nurse or doctor that needed to give permission.

Other patients wanted to be alone when they died. Perhaps they didn't want their loved ones to see them take their last breath. Or maybe they were just private or solitary by nature. Again, death often allowed this.

A few patients seemed to have been granted the power to delay their passing until a specific moment or event. Some waited until a specific family member was or wasn't present. Others waited for their parish priest or minister to bless them before they died.

As health care professionals, when someone was dying, we often tried all of these things to help in the dying process. We announced certain visitors. We gave permission. We told family members to give permission. We tried it all.

* * *

Ruby came to the ER after falling as she was leaving church. On admission to the ICU, she told us she didn't remember what had happened. She'd gone to the church to see her granddaughter, who was a bridesmaid in a wedding. She remembered walking out but the only thing she recalled after that was being in an ambulance.

In the ER, she assured her family she was fine and insisted they go back to the wedding. Everyone did but her son and her daughter-in-law. Her daughter-in-law worked as a registered nurse at that very hospital. She was off-duty to attend the wedding but we all knew her and we were surprised to see her sitting out in the waiting room wearing a fancy dress and heels instead of her uniform and comfortable flat white shoes.

"Can they come in yet?" Ruby asked as we moved her to the ICU bed.

"Where are your son and daughter-in-law now?"

"Out in the waiting room."

We told her we'd allow them in as soon as we completed her admission process and got her settled in. Our shift was beginning and Ruby had arrived just as we were coming out of shift report.

During admission, Ruby spoke incessantly about her granddaughter, Joan—how beautiful she looked as a bridesmaid, how nice she was, how close they were. But before we'd finished our admission process, Ruby suddenly began a grand mal seizure. Her body went stiff and trembled. Then she went limp and unresponsive. We could not rouse her.

Although we never found out what caused the original fall, Ruby was now having a hemorrhagic stroke. A blood vessel inside her brain had ruptured and she was bleeding into the brain tissue. One of the nurses ran out into the waiting room to tell Ruby's son and daughter-in-law while the rest of us worked with the physician to assess the damage the bleed had caused to Ruby's brain functions.

"She's got a Babinski reflex," the doctor said. "And she's posturing."

When there's normal neurological function in an adult, the patient's toes will curl down when the bottom of the foot is stroked. When function's impaired, the toes fan out. This is known as a Babinski reflex. Posturing meant the patient's arms and legs became rigid and rotated inward, another abnormal finding.

The doctor announced these findings so we would all know that Ruby's neurological function was gravely impaired.

Ruby's son and daughter-in-law were brought to the bedside. They seemed to be in shock. Ruby had just been talking and laughing with them a few minutes ago. It was difficult for them to see her this way.

Ruby began having more seizures. While we cared for her, the doctor took her son and daughter-in-law to a conference room to discuss the diagnosis and our very limited treatment options. Her family didn't want her to suffer. There was no hospice unit in the facility at that time, so they asked us to just keep her as comfortable as possible. The doctor told the son and daughter-in-law that Ruby was probably not going to make it through the evening.

Her son and daughter-in-law went back to the bedside and cried. We tried to comfort them. After her daughter-in-law had regained her composure, she said she was going back to the wedding. Ruby's son would stay with her.

The daughter-in-law said she would get in touch with Ruby's other son and she would tell the rest of the family about Ruby's condition at the reception. She reassured her husband she would wait until the dinner and dancing ended before she shared the news with Ruby's granddaughter. "She's going to be upset when she finds out and I don't want to ruin her evening. There's nothing she can do anyway."

Ruby's daughter-in-law left and, in a short time, Ruby's other son joined his brother at her side. They both told Ruby it was okay for her to die.

Those who need permission often wait until all their children can say their goodbyes. Ruby had permission from her two sons but she was still hanging on.

Over the next few hours, we watched Ruby breathe, thinking each breath might be her last. "It's okay," her sons reassured her. They hated watching her suffer and were relieved when the meds we were giving stopped the seizures. "She looks peaceful now," one said.

Family members and close friends came to say their goodbyes, many still in semi-formal attire. Her grandson came in his tuxedo. Her daughter-in-law returned, still in her formal dress. Each told Ruby it was okay for her to leave them. They were ready. They said their goodbyes. They gave their permissions. But she hung on.

It was near the end of the shift and we were all amazed that Ruby was still with us. "She's just not ready," my coworker assured her family.

Then we got a call: a visitor wanted to enter. It was Ruby's granddaughter, Joan. We opened the ICU doors and led her to her grandmother's bedside. She was still in her long apricot bridesmaid gown, an apricot silk flower in her hair above her right ear. She rushed to her grandmother.

Joan held back tears as she held Ruby's hand and kissed her on the forehead. She whispered to her and held her close. It was then that Ruby decided it was time.

She died in the embrace of her only granddaughter.

* * *

I've seen many people die. I've seen them suffer for days and weeks and years before dying. Once a patient becomes unconscious, it's impossible for him to tell healthcare providers what he does and doesn't want. We're left to guess.

Ruby was lucky. Her daughter-in-law, a nurse, understood the benefits and burdens of end of life care. She didn't want Ruby to suffer. She was able to help her husband and his brother make informed decisions about treatment. But not all patients are that lucky, and not all families are that fortunate.

No matter how educated or intelligent a layman may be, he or she may not have much knowledge about medicine or nursing. That makes end of life decision-making difficult. Would his mother want us to try everything? Would she want to be intubated and hooked up to a ventilator? Would she want CPR? Or would she just want to be kept comfortable, as she spent time with her family and made the transition from life to death?

It's impossible to know what a person wishes about his or her death unless it is discussed. This is why I became an advocate for living wills and advance directives. These documents allow the living to make their wishes clear about dying.

In 1990, Congress passed the Patient Self Determination Act. More commonly known as the PSDA, this legislation makes it mandatory for health care facilities to provide information and education on advance directives to patients upon admission to the facility. A simple form allows a patient to indicate what treatments she would and would not want if she were to become terminally ill and unable to communicate her desires to the health care team.

Yet, years later, most people still haven't completed and placed on record these important documents. I am glad I did. I don't know when or how I will die, but at least my significant others won't have to worry about how to help me make my transition from life to death—whatever that transition entails. And I hope that I, like Ruby, will be able to make that passage with those special to me, at my side.

The man's body is sacred and the woman's body is sacred,
No matter who it is, it is sacred — is it the meanest one in the laborers' gang?

– from "I Sing the Body Electric" by Walt Whitman

Eleven
BODY BAG:
The Body after Death

It was nearly two in the afternoon and the second time the pager had gone off for the morgue. As supervisor, it was my responsibility to respond, so I excused myself from the conversation I was having with the staff and hurried down the back steps to the thick glass doors. I pressed a button that swung them open and let in the lanky funeral director.

"Rose Tyler." He didn't look at me as he made this announcement in the raspy voice of a smoker. His thin body was hunched over the gurney as he wheeled it across the tiled floor.

Tick a tick a tick a tick a tick tick tick tick a tick.

I led the way. Keys clanked as I stood before the wide wooden doors, trying to locate the gold-toned key for the morgue. It was dull from use and someone had printed an "M" on it with a black sharpie. Unfortunately, every other key on the ring was a dull gold-tone also, and several had other black letters printed on them.

By the time I found it I was flustered. I fumbled as I slid the key into the slot and unlocked the double doors. Inside, the air was cool and laced with the strong odor of formaldehyde. Everything took on a sickly shade of green except for the funeral director's skin, which remained the same pale gray as his eyes and hair.

I opened the top cooler and checked the toe tag on the corpse. Wrong patient. Second cooler. Wrong. Third. Fourth. Fifth. Sixth.

I pivoted on my white sneakers and leaned back against the cold metal of the cooler. "Mrs. Tyler's not here," I reluctantly reported.

The funeral director's hands flew up to his face. His head dropped into the bowl formed by long crooked fingers. His head swung from side to side. His body rocked. Muffled words were all that came through tight lips.

His growing impatience made me nervous. Inside my pocket was a paper with my notes from the morning report. I fumbled around before removing it, unfolding it, and checking it for any further information I could garner about Mrs. Tyler. "She died a little after eight this morning. Let me call the unit."

As I called, the thin man paced behind me grumbling about the importance of refrigeration. I could hear only part of his sentences. "Her skin's going to turn black. It's going to slough off during embalmment."

I tried to ignore him so I could concentrate on locating Mrs. Tyler's body, which I did manage at last. "The body's still in the room. I'll page the orderly to bring her down."

"I'm not waiting. It's been long enough." He pushed the gurney in front of him as he stomped past me and made his way through the hallways.

Tick a tick a tick a tick a tick tick tick tick a tick.

I trailed behind. "Sir, you can't go onto the unit with a body bag. There are other patients and visitors. It's not allowed."

He pretended not to hear me as I continued pleading my case. I raced behind him toward the patient's room.

As we entered the room assigned to Mrs. Tyler, we were met with the unpleasant stench of baked chicken, mashed potatoes and corn all mixed together with the odor of steamed plastic. Then we both halted, staring. Not only was Rose Tyler still in her bed, her dead body was positioned upright with a lunch tray on the over-bed table in front of her.

The director immediately began a new oration about rigor mortis as he fumbled with buttons and knobs, trying to put down the head of the bed. But once the mattress was flat, he discovered that the body had stiffened in the sitting position. He tried to reposition it. He placed his slender fingers on her shoulders and urged her torso toward the bed.

For some reason, I didn't even offer to help. I simply moved the food tray and over-bed table out of his way. Then I stood in shock watching what looked like a teeter totter with Rose Tyler's head on one end and her feet on the other. The funeral director, with teeth clenched, pushed her shoulders toward the mattress. But as her head lowered, her feet rose into the air. He tugged her legs down and her head rocked upward again. Head down, feet up. Feet down, head up. Up. Down. Up. Down. But he didn't give up.

I clasped my hand over my mouth and stared in disbelief. The funeral director complained and complained. He moaned and groaned. He tugged on the body bag. He pulled and struggled with the black plastic. He yanked harder. He heaved and wrenched until the bag finally stretched around the misaligned corpse.

Finally, I felt obligated to help. I tugged on the heavy brass zipper in an attempt to close the bag. I pulled the edges of black plastic as close together as possible, then struggled to hold them together with one hand while my other hand yanked on the tarnished zipper's slider body. Align and pull. Align and pull, until finally, the slider crunched up along the zipper's teeth. Slowly, the zipper curved in various directions, making its way over the stiffened legs that jutted out from the sack. Right to left, under and over, all the way to the top stop. A feeble "sorry about this" was all I could manage to get out.

He didn't look at me. He just grunted.

We were successful. We'd closed the bag. I took a step back from the bed and let out a long exhalation. Then I stood and watched the gangly funeral director wheel the gurney and the oddly shaped body bag down the hall.

Tick a tick a tick a tick a tick tick tick tick a tick.

* * *

I was flabbergasted that day and for quite a while afterward. As time went by, I found myself laughing when I remembered that day. Even more recently, when I would tell this story, I'd have a hard time doing so without giggling. Not because I disrespect the deceased body, but because I'm not sure how else to deal with the bizarre chain of events and what we did.

As I read Mary Roach's *Stiff: The Curious Life of Human Cadavers*, stories of autopsies, embalming, and cremations, I found myself chuckling. I told myself this shouldn't be funny; that death and the bodies She leaves behind are serious matters. Yet I'm still laughing, and this makes me stop to ponder why I'm so amused.

I've heard it said that to really know oneself, a person has to be able to laugh at his or her own foibles. This shows strength of character. The same is said about relationships.

When we truly know someone, we accept the flaws and idiosyncracies. Laughing (though not too gleefully) at our loved ones' quirks is a sign of endearment.

Perhaps we could say the same about Death. To know Her on an intimate level is to be able to laugh at Her curious nature. Those of us who've seen death up close and personal can't let ourselves be ruled by Her morbidity. Otherwise, we'd never be able to sleep or care or love again. In a way, by facing Death and interacting so familiarly with Her, we've earned the right to laugh.

Creeds and schools in abeyance,
Retiring back a while sufficed at what they are, but never forgotten,
I harbor for good or bad, I permit to speak at every hazard,
Nature without check with original energy.

– from "Song of Myself" by Walt Whitman

Twelve
SO MUCH LIKE HER:
Legacies of the Dead

When my son Paul John began kindergarten he, like every other boy, developed friendships. By the end of the year, he had two best friends, Dino and Kevin. The three fair-haired, fair-skinned boys made a unique trio, for both Dino and Kevin stood close to a foot taller than my son.

Like most other parents, I got acquainted with the parents of my son's friends. I figured that if he was going to be spending time with other families, I wanted him to be safe. After all, I'd heard enough horror stories. And as a nurse, I had seen enough cases of neglect and abuse in the ER to fill my head with fears of what could happen. He could climb a tree, fall, break his neck and be paralyzed. He could be shot playing with guns from an unlocked cabinet. He could choke on a toy and no one would know how to do abdominal thrusts. He could be watching pornography. The list of possibilities was forever growing.

So I got to know Dino's parents and Kevin's and I felt secure when Paul John was with either. And as my experiences with these families grew, I came to expect that Paul John's friends' parents would treat my son like they treated their own.

What I didn't expect was the life-altering lessons I would learn from Dino's mom. In the process of getting to know Angela, I learned she had cancer. It had started in the breast, but had metastasized into her brain. Although it was never discussed, as a nurse I knew this was incurable. Angela was dying.

This stark reality reminded me that one day, my son would go through the same thing I went through when my friend's mother had died. I hoped I would know what to do to help him through it when the time came. But until then, I focused on getting him through her illness and explaining to him all the things I wished people would have explained to me.

Looking at Angela, you would never guess she had cancer and was dying. When the rest of the parents showed up at the school to pick up their children looking haggard from the day they were leaving behind, Angela looked radiant. Her strawberry blond hair was never out of place. Her skin was always glowing. There was never a line, clump or smudge in her makeup. She put us to shame. And since most of the other parents at the school knew of her chemotherapy, radiation and stereotaxic surgeries, most people made an effort to approach her and tell her how wonderful she looked.

* * *

Like most children, mine were continuously asking for playtime with their friends. I would often answer the phone to hear Dino's prepubescent voice. "Can Paul John come over my house to play?"

I would always be reluctant to agree. While I had no problem entrusting my son to the care of Dino's parents, I wondered if his mother might be too tired to put up with overactive boys. The boys could never spend an extended period on any one activity. Instead, they would hunt down a parent every half hour or so asking permission to engage in one thing or another. "Can we ride bikes?" "Can we build a tent in the back yard?" "Can we make pizza for lunch?" "Can we watch TV?" "Can we build a campfire and roast marshmallows?"

I would thank Angela for the invitation and offer to have the kids come to my house instead. But Angela would insist and soon we would come to realize that no matter how tired or sick, she enjoyed having them around. Perhaps it added normalcy to her life.

The amazing part of it all was my son's response to the situation.

"Was Dino's mom feeling okay today?" I would ask when he would come home.

He would often tell me that she'd had to stay in bed for the day. But he would add with excitement, "We put her lunch on a tray and got to take it up to her."

We got to take it up to her. Those words would resound in my head. He didn't whine. He didn't complain. In fact, the opposite. He looked at being able to help his friend's mother as a privilege, as something he felt proud to be able to do, something he wanted to do. This amazed me and I felt proud of my son for caring, but part of me still worried that the boys' being in her house all day might be too taxing for Angela.

But when I would ask if my son was being a nuisance, Angela would protest, "I don't know what I would do without those boys." That's just how she was.

One of my favorite stories about Angela involved a summer trip to Camp Acahela. Paul John, Dino, and Kevin were all active Cub Scouts and, as is customary in scouting, they spent a week camping. At the end of the week, the parents were invited to join the boys for the day. We would have dinner together in the mess hall and then the Scouts would put on a show for us before ending the day with a campfire celebration.

Since Kevin's father was a chaperone at the camp, Kevin's mother, Carol, and I decided to drive to the campgrounds together. I drove my gold minivan and Carol played copilot, directing me through the rural roads. Carol's other son, Jason, and my twin daughters sat in the back seat, amused by a video on the small screen above them.

After a long drive on back roads, we arrived in the dirt parking lot at the campground and drove around, grumbling about the lack of spaces. "I guess we're going to have to walk," we whined as we parked the van at the far end. And we complained when we stepped out into the hot, humid, mosquito-infested air.

We trudged across the rocky ground with Jason and my daughters close behind. We continued our peevish snit as we climbed the grassy hill to the mess hall. Once there, we whined and squawked to anyone who would listen. "The parking's so far away. It's so hot up here. These mosquitoes are annoying."

We were in the middle of one of our rants when Angela approached us. We stopped immediately. She'd spent the previous week in the intensive care unit. She'd undergone another stereotaxic surgery to remove additional malignant tissue from her brain and spent her recovery period on a ventilator. But here she was, looking healthy and happy as she offered her arm to her mother and helped her across the bumpy lawn.

Carol and I sat on a bench made from a tree trunk as Angela and her mom climbed the hill toward us. The two red headed women, dressed in white Keds and denim

Capri pants, smiled as they held on to each other. With their youthful faces, they looked more like sisters than a mother and daughter.

Then her mother lost her balance and fell. Angela toppled on top of her. We all gasped and rushed to help, but Angela, true to form, simply stood and brushed the grass off. "I'm fine," she assured everyone and then laughed at herself.

Carol and I sat back on the log bench. "That's the last time I'll complain about walking up a hill," Carol whispered.

* * *

As the years passed and we watched Angela face her fate with courage, we learned to be more tolerant, more patient, and more forgiving. And we were all in awe of her ability to be positive despite the pain, fatigue, and nausea that so frequently plagued her. Her sense of humor was contagious.

She was a hockey fan and, if she had her way, she would never miss going to see our local AHL farm team, the Wilkes-Barre/Scranton Penguins. I would see her at the games in her wheelchair with her morphine pump on her lap and a colorful afghan wrapped around her.

At the end of one game, I accompanied her to the ladies' room. She wheeled herself into the stall marked for the handicapped and I waited for her near a row of white ceramic sinks. We were the only two left inside the restroom when I heard her call my name with a small chuckle.

"I'm still here," I assured her.

"I'm so embarrassed," she said. "But I can't get up."

"Okay. Unlock the door and I'll help you."

"I can't. I can't reach the door."

She giggled as I shimmied along the floor and under the metal door of the stall. I joined in her laughter as I helped her off the commode and back into her wheelchair.

It was amazing how she could turn an embarrassing moment into a fun-filled memory. But it was heartbreaking to watch the cancer weaken her. I recognized the signs of impending death. She was losing weight, she was always tired, she was unusually pale.

It was the summer after our boys completed the fifth grade when the cancer finally caused Angela to be bed-ridden. There were too many tumors and nothing more her doctors could do. She was a nurse. I was a nurse. We both knew the time had come to stop treatment. Unlike me, she accepted it graciously. After a brief hospital stay, she was transferred to a hospice unit.

We'd planned to visit her on a Sunday, but that changed when we got a call Saturday afternoon. I was working in the garden when it came. I brushed dirt off my hands and answered.

"Hi Joyce. It's Carol. I just came from visiting Angela. If you want to see her, you need to go there today. They don't expect her to make it to tomorrow."

I left the rake in the dirt, along with the basket of weeds I had pulled. I washed up as quickly as I could and took my son to see his best friend's mother. I'd had six years to prepare but somehow I wasn't prepared at all.

As I entered the room, I avoided looking at the bed. I said hello to Angela's mother, who was sitting near the foot of the bed. I forced a smile for Angela's husband. He was sitting on the edge at Angela's side. I swallowed hard as I finally worked up the nerve to turn my eyes to Angela.

It was hard to see her lying still in a semi-fetal position. Her face was gaunt and pale. Her lips were so white they

123

blended with the chalky pallor of her face. She didn't move. It seemed so abnormal because no matter how sick she was, she'd always managed a smile. But there in the hospice unit, she didn't open her eyes. She didn't move a muscle. It didn't even seem as if it could really be her. It was more like an empty shell made to look like Angela. But it was her and I needed to remind myself that this would be the last time I would see her.

I put my hand on Paul John's shoulder and gently guided him closer. He leaned over and gave her a kiss on the cheek. I cried as I watched him say goodbye, then cried even harder as I did the same.

The following morning was the Fourth of July and we were hosting the customary cookout and fireworks at our house later that day. Just a few moments after I'd crawled out of bed, the phone rang. Dino's voice came through the receiver. *"My mom died this morning."*

It took a few seconds for me to absorb the news and he waited on the other end in silence. "I'm so sorry" was all I could manage. After a few deep breaths, I asked him how he was doing.

"I'm good. Is Paul John up yet?"

I told him that Paul John was sleeping and offered to wake him.

"That's okay."

"I'll have him call back as soon as I wake him and tell him about your mom."

"Okay."

I invited him to come to our house while his dad went about planning her funeral. Then I went to my son's room to tell him the news.

I sat on the edge of Paul John's bed and placed my hand on his back. He was spread out across the mattress with his face down in his pillow. I took a moment to collect my thoughts before I called his name. No matter how many times I've had to deliver such news, it had never gotten easier. And the fact that I was delivering it to my own twelve-year-old made it all the more difficult. I took a deep breath.

"Pon." I shook him as I repeated his nickname before he squinted up.

I swallowed hard to stop my voice from cracking and shaking. I told him Dino had just called. "His mom died this morning." I started to cry despite my efforts not to.

"Where is he?"

"Home. But I offered to let him to come over."

"Can he?"

"I don't know."

We both sat on his bed in silence for a moment or two and then I excused myself, both to give him the privacy to grieve and to give myself a moment alone to cry yet again.

* * *

I felt some degree of comfort when Dino called back and took me up on my invitation. In some odd way, it made me feel useful. Being able to take care of Angela's son made me feel I'd found some way to help at a time when I knew of no other way to console him. As a nurse, it was important for me to feel as though I could do *something*.

Despite my sadness over the loss of my friend, I forged on with our celebration that afternoon. Dino joined us for our cookout and was able to stay around for our fireworks display. I remember sitting on the front porch watching the boys as they set off bottle rockets.

It seemed unreal that they could be having such fun. Perhaps they knew more about death than I. I wondered if maybe life had made me forget that death could be peaceful and natural. Maybe I'd grown jaded by my experiences. Maybe I needed to look to them to see what life and death were really about.

I simply sat and watched the boys.

The snap of a rocket, and the smell of gunpowder. Dino ran to me and smiled. "This is the best Fourth of July ever," he yelled. A large grin spread across his smooth face.

I couldn't help but smile back.

* * *

At times since then, I find myself wallowing in self-pity. I can't call my dad and invite him for a coffee. I can't call my old friend to ask if she's going to the class reunion. It's then that I stop and remember Angela and Dino. I remind myself how Angela lived her life and how she faced dying. I can still see her smiling, and I can't help but smile too.

I felt a Funeral, in my Brain,
And Mourners to and fro
Kept treading – treading - till it seemed
That Sense was breaking through –
And when they all were seated,
A Service, like a Drum –
Kept beating – beating - till I thought
My mind was going numb –
And then I heard them lift a Box
And creak across my Soul
With those same Boots of Lead, again,
Then Space - began to toll,
As all the Heavens were a Bell,
And Being, but an Ear,
And I, and Silence, some strange Race
Wrecked, solitary, here –
And then a Plank in Reason, broke,
And I dropped down, and down –
And hit a World, at every plunge,
And Finished knowing – then –

– from "I Felt a Funeral, In My Brain" by Emily Dickinson.

Thirteen
A NOT SO CHRISTMAS CAROL:
Suicide

Maybe I'd watched too many episodes of *ER*. Why else would I sign up to work in the emergency room? I already had a position as a hospital-based educator, so it wasn't like I needed to. But the manager was a friend and she was always telling me how short staffed they were. I looked at it as both a favor to her and a way to keep up my clinical skills.

The anticipated glamor was quickly extinguished. Where were the doctors like George Clooney's Doug Ross? What happened to all the vivid scenes where blood squirts everywhere? Why didn't we have as many staff members as they had on television shows?

The real emergency room was nowhere near as dramatic. Treatments were routine and patients lumped together in my mind, usually filed by their diagnosis. All the heart attacks went in one memory file, the strokes in another, the rashes in another, the asthma in another. But every once in a while, a patient stood out and got a file of his own. For me, that was Johnny.

The day Johnny came in started as a routine day. Buzzers sounded in patient rooms, phones rang at the nurses' station, staff members zipped up and down hallways in scrubs and lab coats, and the scent of urine permeated the air from the utility room. Things were normal.

Then the scanner at the desk buzzed and we were alerted an ambulance would shortly be arriving with a sixteen-year-old victim of a suicide attempt. Within a few minutes, two other nurses and I stood at the bedside with the on-duty physician, ready to meet the patient.

In a blur of navy blue, uniformed emergency medical technicians and paramedics came rushing through the glass doors of the ambulance bay and down the hallway toward us. They spouted words and acronyms that sounded like a defunct ancient language. I didn't listen. At least I didn't register any of it. Instead, my eyes and my thoughts focused on the patient.

Johnny's youthful face bore an expression of hopelessness. His cheekbones were obscured by the swelling in his pale cheeks. His dry purplish lips were parted. Angst radiated from him like a brownish green aura. One of the paramedics unhooked the strap of the cervical collar. As he lifted it from the skin, we all glanced at the red and purple line that marked where the rope had bruised him.

The physician I'd been working with all morning gave a quick nod and the paramedic replaced the white plastic collar and secured it once again around Johnny's neck. Then he ordered the rest of the ambulance crew to stop CPR and they dropped away leaving the small blue bag attached to the tube that jutted from his mouth. We silently began performing the tasks we were trained to perform in situations like this one.

Another nurse and I log rolled Johnny onto his side and held him there while a third nurse slid a blue paper sheet under his buttocks to protect the bed. The physician inserted a gloved finger into Johnny's rectum. Brown mushy feces poured out onto the sheet and we lowered our heads. We knew what it meant when the patient had lost his rectal tone. His suicide had been successful. His neck had snapped as he'd kicked the chair out from underneath himself. A break that high on the spinal column severed the cord at a level that caused transmission of all impulses to stop and his bodily functions, including breathing, had ceased. At that point, nothing could have been done to save him.

The doctor shook his bowed head. "D.O.A.," he announced before glancing at the clock and noting the time.

The paramedics and EMTs gathered their paraphernalia. Though we knew each other from our years of working together, no one said a word. It was a rare and awkward silence. In the distance, buzzers and phones continued to ring. The ping of equipment and clomp of shoes could be heard as the crew headed back out to their vehicle.

One of the nurses took her papers off to the station to put together the chart, while another accompanied the physician out to the waiting room where they would tell Johnny's family. I stood alone with Death.

Pressure filled my chest and worked its way up my neck as I fought back tears and tried to focus on the tasks at hand. I filled a basin with water at the sink and began the post mortem care. First, all attempts of resuscitation were removed and discarded. I loosened the tape and slid the endotracheal tube out from Johnny's mouth. I peeled dressings off and took the intravenous line out of the vein in his arm.

The crackle echoed around the room as I pulled the Velcro straps apart then removed the immobilization collar from Johnny's neck. Then I took a white washcloth and began cleaning Johnny's body, wishing that I could wash away the putrid odor of dead flesh. As I ran the cloth over his eyelids and cheeks, I looked once again at Johnny's teenage face.

Visions of the garden I had visited during my near-death experience flashed in my mind. For the first time, I felt gratitude I'd survived. This amplified the sorrow brought on by Johnny's death. I found myself wishing that life could be like Charles Dickens's *A Christmas Carol* and I could be the Ghost of Christmas Future. In my mind, I took Johnny by the hand and led him through a burst of fog until we were a few years ahead in time. He was twenty and was sitting on the bench of his college campus. A young woman plopped down next to him. She looked at Johnny and her grin nearly made the corners of her mouth touch her earlobes.

"You look good in blue," he told her.

A rosy pink engulfed her face like a lampshade when the bulb is suddenly turned on. They basked in a moment of intimate silence before she whispered, "Thank you."

"You're welcome!" he answered.

He laid kisses on her forehead. She dropped her head onto his shoulder.

I imagined that as I played out this fictional scene of his future, Johnny rolled his eyes and let out a groan. He couldn't see it as I did. He knew his past. He knew the events that led up to his tragic death. I could only envision them.

In my imaginary scene, he tugged my arm and whisked me backward in time. Into his past.

He was twelve and we entered his house through the kitchen. His mother and father were at the table, too involved in an argument to have noticed his entrance. He led me through the family room.

His older brother was lying on the couch watching the television. "Get out of my way, ya dork," he yelled as he craned around us without taking his eyes off the show.

Johnny ignored him and took me upstairs to his room, where he spent most of his time in an uncomfortable solitude. Band posters adorned the walls, but the cabinets and shelves looked empty with no photographs or trophies or other memorabilia. He pointed at his backpack and I saw that someone has written "You Suck" on it with a black magic marker. Johnny just stood there with his head down and his hands in his pockets.

I closed my eyes and in an instant we were back in the present. We were back to the reality of the emergency room with its buzzing and beeping and ammonia smell. Despite the fluorescent overhead lighting, the room felt dark and cold, even chilling.

I stood at the side of the gurney where Johnny's body lay. Muted shades of purple, red and blue slowly worked their way over the milky white skin until they covered his arms and legs.

I finished cleaning the stiff, mottling body and covered it with a fresh white sheet, revealing only his youthful face. As I arranged the sheet to cover the rope burn on his neck, I stared once again at the sadness in his dead eyes. My hopes for his future collided with the stark realities of whatever had been his past, and we were left with nothing but the present. He was hopeless and I was helpless. There we were—alone—just Johnny and I.

* * *

Every time I read obituaries of young men or women who died unexpectedly at home, I wonder if it was suicide. And what led up to their despair. Bullying? Addiction?

Bankruptcy? Loneliness? Personal failure? If only someone could have reassured them that they matter, given them hope for the future. If only they'd called the suicide prevention hotline.

And how must their parents feel? I admit, I can't imagine. Just the thought of losing one of my own makes me sick and ill at ease. True, I don't know the people I'm reading about. They're just names and pictures in the paper. But still, I think about them and I weep.

What do you think has become of the women and children?

They are alive and well somewhere;

The smallest sprouts show there is really no death,

And if ever there was it led forward life, and does not wait

at the end to arrest it,

And ceased the moment life appeared.

– from "A Child Said, What Is The Grass?" by Walt Whitman

Fourteen
SLEEPLESS:
Sudden Infant Death Syndrome (SIDS)

My phone buzzed at 6:32 a.m. Though I was awake, I was startled. As with every early morning or late night call or text, my heart stopped for a split second. I was always worried it would be terrible news. I said a quick prayer that my three children were safe in their beds. One was in his room across the hall but the other two were in their apartments near the universities they were attending.

When I finally got the nerve to look at my cell, a friend's name was on the screen. The text notified me and a few other friends that his cousin's baby had died. The baby was two months old. SIDS, I thought, and said another prayer—this one for the baby and his family.

I got up and peered into my son's room. The memory quilt made from his old t-shirts was draped over him and I watched it rise and fall with each breath. I went back into my room and grabbed my phone. I sent a text to each of my daughters. *Good morning!* I couldn't proceed with my day with a clear mind until I got their replies.

* * *

Everyone jokes that my children didn't really sleep through the night since they were six weeks old. They say I was just too lazy to get out of bed. They say they were probably up crying all night but I slept through it.

I go along because I know it's just not true. (That is the part about being too lazy. All three of my children really did sleep through the night since they were six weeks old.) The truth is, I got up many times each night. I needed to make sure they were breathing.

I had SIDS-a-phobia. I was petrified that I would find my child dead in the crib. This was not irrational. I'd seen it and it was unforgettable.

Nothing would cure me of my phobia until my children were over six months old—the age where the risk finally becomes very low. I'm not sure I'm cured even now.

* * *

I'll never forget the first time I saw an infant whose cause of death was Sudden Infant Death Syndrome, or simply SIDS. I'd been a registered nurse for less than a year. I worked on a unit that treated adults, so death and children wasn't an association I made readily. Sure, I'd heard about it. I'd studied it as a nursing student. But I never really knew anyone who had a child die of SIDS and I'd never seen a dead baby in my entire twenty-one years.

It was my day off and I'd planned to go shopping with my mother just like I did on every other free day. But first I had to go to the hospital to pick up my paycheck. (This was before direct deposit.) I was dressed up in a white blouse and denim skirt. I would pick up my check, take it to the bank and cash it. Then I would have money to spend on my shopping spree.

I walked into the paneled lobby and approached the marble desk that took up one whole wall. The top was enclosed in glass and I had to wait for the clerk to slide it open and ask what she could do for me.

"I'm here to pick up my check."

"Have a seat."

I sat in one of the faux leather chairs, one that faced the glass wall that looked out at the street. I could also see the ambulance bay and the parking lot.

"Supervisor, call the operator. Supervisor, call the operator," I heard announced overhead.

I hoped the supervisor wasn't busy so that she would come with my check quickly. The place wasn't very big, only fifty beds. It shouldn't take her long. So I sat in the chair and looked around. I noticed a scuff on my favorite white shoes (the ones with the silver and turquoise trim). I tried wiping it off with my finger, to no avail.

I lifted my head and relaxed back into the chair. Letting out a sigh, I turned my focus to the view. I looked out into the late spring sky. Before my thoughts could wander to shopping, I noticed a woman running up the street toward the hospital. She appeared to be carrying something. I stood and walked to the window. Is that a blanket or a doll, or . . .

My rambling thoughts came to a halt. "Oh my God," I said aloud. She was carrying a baby – a stiff, dead baby.

I forgot about my check and ran down the hallway toward the ER. The clomping of my shoes must have startled the nurse, Holly, and she poked her head out and blinked at me inquisitively.

"There's a woman running up the street toward the hospital with a dead baby," I told her as I tried to catch my breath.

I repeated my statement as she bolted to the window and looked out. She ran past me to call the emergency room physician, then past me again as she went back to the door to meet the woman. "Call a code," Holly yelled at the receptionist as she darted past her.

I suppose my cheeks had lost all color and the receptionist probably was wondering if I was the one who needed the medical care. She stared at me as she lifted the black receiver from the cradle.

Within seconds, everything was happening at once. The woman with the cradled bundle burst through the ER doors screaming, "Help me. Help my baby!"

Members of the code team were zipping past me with hurried steps. Housekeeping and maintenance personnel were gathering in the hallway, peering in through the open door and whispering to each other.

From the hallway, I could see people in white uniforms and drab green scrubs surrounding the exam table. A nurse came out and took the baby's mother into a quiet room across the hall. The physician was spouting orders. "Give an epi! Put a tube in. Try a 4.5."

I didn't know what he was talking about but the nurses did. They were taking things out of the bright red crash cart that stood at the head of the gurney. The baby lay on the gurney. It was so small the gurney was more sheet than body. This was different than what I was used to. With adults you could barely see the sheets underneath their bodies. I just kept staring and thinking about how tiny the patient was.

Things were happening fast and steady and I was so intent on watching the flurry of activity that I was actually startled when the supervisor called my name and touched my arm. "Come with me," she said softly, "I'll get your check."

I followed her down the hallway, back toward the main lobby. She led me into an office, where she opened a safe, removed my check from a stack of envelopes, and handed it to me. "I have to get over to the ER," she told me. "Have a good day."

She led me out and pulled the door shut before rushing past. I stood in her wake for a moment, still picturing the tiny body on the long white sheet. I started walking but instead of heading out to my car, I took a slow walk back to the ER.

It had been forty-five minutes since I'd seen the woman running down the street toward us. As I approached the emergency room, the physician was leaving. He strolled past me into the room across the hall where the nurse had taken the mother. The health care team filed out with the same expressions as a team that's just lost a hard game.

I found Holly. "Did the baby make it?"

She looked at me sympathetically, "It was SIDS."

I was perplexed. She must have seen I didn't comprehend her reply. "Sudden Infant Death Syndrome," she stated emphatically.

I knew what the acronym stood for. I just wanted an answer to my question. So, I repeated it, "Did the baby make it?"

She furrowed her brow. "The D stands for death. Sudden Infant Death Syndrome." When she said the words this time, she emphasized the word death.

I'd never thought of it that way. I had to take a moment to absorb the concept.

"Once the baby dies," she explained. "There's nothing we can do."

"But." The word slipped out of my mouth with no other words to follow.

Holly managed a smile, "Oh, that." She looked toward where just a few moments before the health care team had worked so diligently. "That's for us," she said. After a pause, she added, "And for the mother."

The words stuck in my head like the words to a song. A song that would play over and over again until one day, the lyrics would make sense.

* * *

Sadly, I'd seen SIDS again when I worked in an emergency room years later.

That time, I was standing in a reception area in the emergency department with another nurse, Ellen, and Dr. Mack. We were planning schedules. Ironically, we were looking through the staff list to determine who needed to attend the next Advanced Cardiac Life Support and Pediatric Advanced Life Support training sessions, known more commonly as ACLS and PALS. Everyone who worked in the ER was required to complete training and retraining in basic or advanced life support for adults and children every year.

An aunt babysitting her nieces and nephews had checked on her four-month-old niece, who was napping in her crib. She noticed the baby was not moving or breathing. Since she was near the hospital, she grabbed the child and ran across the street to us.

We raced to take the baby from her as she burst through the large glass doors of the ambulance bay. We didn't need to ask questions. We had enough experience to know what had happened.

The baby was placed on a gurney and everyone stepped into place around her. We'd all been trained in pediatric life support methods. Sadly, we'd all seen SIDS before, too. We assumed our roles without any formal assignment. One nurse took the baby's aunt into a quiet room. There, she got the details of what had happened leading up to her bringing the baby to us. She had the unpleasant task of getting contact information for the parents and making calls to notify them their baby was with us. She told them where to come without giving too much detail. She didn't tell them their child was already dead.

Our hospital's policy was that death should not be reported over a phone. And though we knew our efforts were futile, the physician had not yet pronounced the baby dead. We continued our resuscitation efforts until the parents arrived. We knew both the health care providers and the parents needed that assurance.

While the nurse talked with the aunt in a quiet room, the rest of us carried out the PALS algorithm. One nurse stood at the baby's feet, wrapped her hands around the baby's tiny torso and compressed the chest with her thumbs.

A respiratory therapist stood at the baby's head. He used a small blue bag with a tiny facemask. The bag was connected to an oxygen tank on the wall with long green tubing. The therapist squeezed the bag every few seconds to push air into the baby's lungs.

Ellen stood to the left. She skillfully started an intravenous catheter in the baby's arm, attaching it to a bag of IV fluid hung on a silver pole near the baby's left shoulder.

Ellen pulled syringes filled with medications from a color-coded bag and administered them based on a preset, timed schedule. The bag was part of a set based on a pediatric emergency measuring tape called a Broselow Chart. When the baby had been first placed on the gurney, Ellen had quickly measured her with the Broselow Tape. She placed the top arrow of the tape at the top of the baby's head and stretched the tape alongside her body. The color of the block where the baby's feet touched determined what color bag we would use for the proper supplies.

The feet fell into the pink block so we used the pink bag. It held airways and medications, supplies and equipment appropriate for a child that size. Having everything prepared ahead of time diminished the risk of making an error during such a stressful event.

Dr. Mack and I stood on the baby's right as he gave orders. "Epinepherine."

"Epinepherine given," Ellen confirmed.

Dr. Mack clicked his pen over and over. He tapped his foot on the tile floor. The sole of his black shoe made a dull thump in a rhythm that mimicked the chest compressions. Every once in a while, he took a white handkerchief from his pocket and wiped the sweat from his tanned forehead and the back of his neck.

I held a clipboard with the resuscitation log. My job was to record everything we did. The log would go into the baby's medical record. I looked at the clock, noted the time the epinephrine was given, and recorded this. It was easier to focus on the clock and the log than it was to look at the baby.

A chaplain arrived wearing black clericals. He anointed the baby at the aunt's request. He made an announcement that if any of us in the room needed to come talk to him about the death, he would be available. He circled the room, placing his hands gently on each of our shoulders, trying to offer some consolation.

At some point, Dr. Mack moved up near the baby's head and placed a small tube into the baby's mouth and down into her airway. This would help the oxygen go into the lungs more easily.

When that tube was in place, Ellen placed another in through the mouth and down into her stomach. This would stop the air from distending her belly.

When the parents arrived, Dr. Mack ended our activity and pronounced the baby dead. He and the chaplain left and took the parents to the quiet room, where the aunt sat waiting.

We removed all of the tubes from the little girl. Ellen brought in a rocking chair from the lounge. When the doctor and the chaplain were finished breaking the news to the parents, Ellen would bring them in and allow the mother to sit in the rocker and hold her baby for the last time.

I've heard more than one mother crying in that chair, cradling her dead child. I couldn't stay to watch. I couldn't wait for the workday to end, so I could go home and hug by own kids.

Pain – has an Element of Blank –
It cannot recollect
When it begun – Or if there were
A time when it was not –

It has no Future – but itself–
Its Infinite contain
Its Past – enlightened to perceive
New Periods – Of Pain.

– from "Pain Has An Element of Blank" by Emily Dickinson

Fifteen
I HATE THE SMELL OF CHRISTMAS:
Dealing with Murder

D id you ever notice that once autumn rolls around, it seems you hear more about death? The leaves fall. Flowers start to die. The grass turns brown and dull. People get old. People get sick. They die.

This idea seems to be widely accepted in the nursing profession. We would say "it's that time of year" whenever we would get a dying patient on our unit. And being able to grasp and accept that seemed expected of nursing students. "If you can't deal with dying," the nurses would say, "you don't belong in nursing."

By the time I got to my final year of school, I'd cared for enough terminal patients to be able to see the trend. Although I'd just turned twenty, I felt comfortable with the concept. I didn't *like* it when someone died, but it seemed that was the logical end to the progression of life.

But up until that point, I hadn't really known death other than as a natural process that followed on advanced age. I'd rarely stopped to think it could occur in other ways too. Sure, there was the occasional car accident, where young adults were killed after celebrating at a graduation party. And there was the teenager found in the woods after an overdose. But even that seemed somewhat natural, because I could rationalize that death was a consequence of an action, wise or not.

The one means of death I never really gave much thought to was murder. It seemed to me that murder was a senseless death. Maybe that's why I was content to limit my notion of homicide to what I read in books and saw in movies and television shows.

My first exposure to murder was *Dark Shadows*. I was only five or six when that show became popular, but since the older kids were watching it, I wasn't going to miss out. Some of the older girls in my neighborhood would gather to watch Jonathan Frid as Barnabas Collins. I would shimmy in between them and watch too.

Barnabas was a vampire. He was a tormented soul released from the family mausoleum. He spent his nights searching for redemption. The show followed his plight, along with that of the witches, warlocks and werewolves that plagued the town of Collinsport. As strange as this may sound, I was mesmerized and actually thought it might be cool to be a vampire.

As I got older, I read about murder in Stephen King novels. It only happened under the most bizarre circumstances (and for some reason, only in the state of Maine).

I do remember reading about one case in our local newspaper. A teenaged boy lured two children into the woods and killed them. This happened within thirty miles of my home and I recall people talking about it. But since I didn't know the teenager or his victims, it didn't seem real.

Thus homicide, deliberate killing, was nothing more than an abstract concept. It happened to actors and actresses on shows like *Hill Street Blues*. One week, I would see the actor lying dead in a pool of blood. The next week, the same actor was sipping a martini on *The Love Boat* or *Fantasy Island*.

That all changed in December of 1984. The holiday was approaching and I began counting down the days until graduation. It was hard to believe that in less than a year, I would be taking the state board exam to become a registered nurse. Once the break came, I would officially be in my last semester of nursing school. This filled me with both eagerness and anxiety.

I got home exhausted from my clinical day at the hospital. After taking a bath and eating supper, I wanted to crawl into bed and sleep. But finals were approaching and I needed to spend some time studying. I got out my books and notes and reviewed them over and over until I could no longer keep my eyes focused on the words.

I must have been in a deep sleep when the phone call came. I have a faint memory of hearing the high-pitched ring, but I must have registered it as part of a dream rather than reality. I vaguely recall my father coming into my room to tell me the news. Of course, I had to have been in a dream state because if I weren't, I most certainly would have reacted. Instead, I processed the occurrence as nothing more than a horrible nightmare.

When my alarm went off early the next morning, I got ready for class. Remnants of the "nightmare" were still on my mind but I tried to push them out of my thoughts. It was still dark out and no one else in the house was awake. There was no one around to tell me the news was real. As I brushed my teeth and pulled my long brown hair into a ponytail, I told myself I'd had a horrific dream, and headed out the door.

Traffic was sparse at that hour. My Chevy Cavalier was stopped in a short line at a traffic signal. The sky was a deep shade of navy blue with no sun or stars. The bright golden light from the arches of the nearby McDonalds reflected off my windshield. The smell of hash browns and coffee filtered into my car. Madonna's new release, "Like a Virgin," had just finished playing on the radio. The news report came on.

I was about to push in a button and switch over to a cassette of *Adam Ant* when Candice's name came through the speaker system. It wasn't a dream. Candice had been bludgeoned and stabbed by her husband. He'd dragged her pregnant body into the woods behind their military base home, then called the authorities and reported her death.

I was frozen in the moment until honking horns startled me out of oblivion. When I looked up, the light had turned green. I somehow managed to push on the accelerator, and maneuvered the car to a classmate's house nearby.

Nursing school and my experiences with death hadn't prepared me for anything like this. I wished there were some sort of textbook that could have outlined what I was supposed to do. I wasn't prepared.

I remember nothing after that moment at the traffic light. It was as though time didn't exist. Reality didn't exist. I know I went to school. I know I went home. But I don't remember any of it.

Perhaps my mind and body tried to block everything out. Maybe they knew that anything they took in could serve as a memory trigger for this atrocious event later. I often think that shock and oblivion are the only defenses against horror. Certainly, they were the coping mechanisms that got me through the days that followed.

The only memory I have of the days between that moment when I heard the news and the moment when I saw Candice's body in the coffin is that of being at my friend Dana's house.

Dana had gone to school with Candice and me from kindergarten through seventh grade. Although she'd graduated from a different high school, she'd always managed to keep in touch. When she heard the news, she called me. We agreed to attend the wake together.

I recall sitting at the table in the kitchen at Dana's parents' house. I stared blankly into space. Dana's mother was baking and I know she spoke to me. I can't recall a word that she said. I just remember sitting there and smelling the warm sugary scent of Christmas cookies baking in the oven. The sweetness made my stomach churn. I don't remember how I stopped myself from vomiting. But I did, and somehow, Dana and I ended up at the funeral home.

Candice wore a white gown. Heavy makeup covered the bruises on her face. She looked innocent and peaceful. I almost expected her to open her big brown eyes and flash one of those huge smiles she was known for in high school.

I knelt and said a prayer. I'm not even sure for what I prayed. Then I turned to her mother and sisters and told them I was sorry.

Through all of it, I remained in a daze. Maybe it was a good thing that my parents had taken me to all of those wakes when I was younger, for now I was able to conduct myself properly with no conscious effort. Maybe my experiences in nursing school were paying off too because to the outside world I must have looked like I was handling it all with courage and poise. But, inside, I was trying to build a house of cards in a windstorm.

I couldn't understand what had happened, how it had happened, or why. She wasn't old. She wasn't sick. She hadn't done anything to cause this.

I was left to re-evaluate everything I'd assumed. Thoughts of Candice's murder had me so preoccupied I barely passed my finals. Too many questions pounded in my head. I needed too many answers that weren't in my books. How could she be gone? How could something like this happen? How does her husband get a chance at probation while I got a life sentence of memories that, when evoked, triggered grief and pain?

Those memories were supposed to be the things that we would joke about at class reunions. Those were the stories we would tell our children and our children's' children.

Now I didn't want those memories. I didn't want to hear the word murder. I didn't want to turn on the television and see the graphic and pseudo-realistic depictions on *Murder She Wrote* and *Miami Vice*. I'd be forced to look at waxy gray body parts strewn inside chalk lines and splotches of darkened red blood splattered on rugs, walls and sidewalks. I'd have to cringe at close-up shots of the victims' horrified faces frozen stiff with their eyes still open. I would have to wonder if that's what Candice had looked like when she'd died.

I didn't want to watch reality TV and broadcastings of murder cases like the OJ Simpson trial. I didn't want to see murder the way it was in the courtroom: tragic images blown up to a size that is three times larger than life and projected onto a screen so that everyone who missed out on the gore at the crime scene could get their fill.

I didn't want to see murder that way. I didn't want to see it as entertainment. I didn't want to see it at all.

I could no longer think of murder as a book or a movie or a television show. When I heard the word, I thought only of the victim. I thought of Candice.

I wondered about her last moments on earth. What was going through her head when she saw the knife? Did she beg for her life, or pray for death? And if both, when was the moment that made her change her mind? I wondered if she'd seen her life pass before her eyes. I wondered if I'd been part of that vision.

Thinking of murder made me not want to think at all. I tried to block out everything that made me think of Candice. I avoided the things that had become triggers for memories of her.

When they played Sister Sledge's "We are Family" during oldies night on the radio, I changed the station because I didn't want to picture her dancing to that song at our junior high school dances. I didn't go to see the remake of *Freaky Friday* because I didn't want to recall I'd watched the original with her. I avoided driving past the elementary school in my hometown because I was afraid I'd see a group of girls giggling on the playground and memories of Candice and me doing that same thing so many years ago would have resurfaced in my mind.

When I heard the word *murder*, I didn't want to think. I didn't want to remember. I turned off every ascending pathway in my nervous system so the outside world could no longer penetrate to the inside. I numbed my heart. I shut my eyes. I closed off my ears. I turned my back on people I loved and on the people who loved me because love required feeling. I transformed myself into a hollow stone statue filled with murdered memories.

The last Night that She Lived
It was a Common Night
Except the Dying –
This to Us
Made Nature different

– from "The Last Night That She Lived" by Emily
Dickinson

Sixteen
DON'T CRY:
More on Murder

Working in both the hospital's education department and the emergency department had its advantages. It was always great to be able to offer an anecdote in a critical care class. And it was rewarding to be able to apply a principle or technique I'd learned in class to the clinical setting.

Many times, I would even get to apply my expertise outside of the hospital. Family members and friends would call looking for advice or reassurance. I liked the fact I was able to provide it. I never realized there would come a time when I wished I didn't have to be "the nurse". And I never thought that after eighteen years of being one that I would be ill prepared. But one November, I learned that when it came to dealing with death, I was really inept.

I grabbed a coffee in the brightly lit hospital cafeteria, hoping it would wake me. I was unaware that caffeine would be completely irrelevant in the day I was about to have. The cream colored walls were brightly lit and adorned with eight by ten sheets of colored paper that announced upcoming events like the Thanksgiving ham and turkey sale and the uniform sale our auxiliary sponsored each year. I walked toward my office offering the required "hellos" to middle managers in business suits and the ever unanswered "how are you" to maintenance men in navy Dickies I passed along the way.

As usual, I was the first to arrive in the office. I flipped on the three light switches, ignoring the one set of lights that would stay off until sometime around ten. It no longer startled us when they suddenly flashed on in the middle of our workday.

The pale pink walls looked dingy and even a mulberry candle failed to suppress the musty smell of the carpet. Raggedy mauve dividers formed cubicles along the perimeter in the shape of upside down "U"s. Mine was the long narrow one on the right.

I took a large gulp of the hot coffee and enjoyed the way it warmed my mouth, throat, and stomach on its way into my system. The little caffeine molecules zipped around my blood stream. They knocked on the cell walls to wake them. They were like microscopic drill sergeants.

Next, I began the Ritual of the Mails. I alternated my attention between the snail mail, inter-office mail, e-mail, and voice mail. It was like a well-rehearsed dance. Turn on computer. Dial in voice mail. Open an interoffice envelope. Click mouse and log onto computer. Enter voice mail password. Read interoffice memo. Open computer mail system. Start first voice mail recording. Open another piece of mail.

I was engrossed when I opened a voice mail from the man that was my husband at the time. *"Joy, it's me. Call me on my cell."*

I looked at the clock and decided the message must be an old one I'd forgotten to delete. I deleted it and moved on to another.

"Hey, girlfriend." I'd just finished my e-mails when I heard my co-worker and friend, Nellie.

I shuffled my feet until they propelled my chair to the opening of my cubicle. "What's up?"

We discussed the day ahead and welcomed our two co-workers, Colleen and Sandy. My phone was ringing, but I ignored it and went into the adjacent classroom, where staff members were beginning to arrive for our 8:00 a.m. in-service on the American Heart Association's Basic Cardiac Life Support for the Health Care Provider, which everyone referred to simply as CPR.

I greeted the class, went through the course objectives and answered a slew of questions, trying to allay the anxieties of the participants.

"What if I kill someone?"

"You can't," I told them. "They're already dead or we wouldn't be doing CPR on them."

"What do I do if it doesn't work?"

"Tell the patient's family."

They looked frightened. I tried to address their concerns. State the death as fact. Keep it simple. Stay calm. Don't cry.

I turned on a video and left them to the digital instructions while I returned to my mail.

There was another message from my husband. *"I thought I'd catch you before class."* A sigh. *"Call me on your break."*

I wondered why he was calling when he was supposed to be driving our kids to school. I deleted the message and planned to call his cell as soon as I finished with the goldenrod envelope I'd just slit open.

I reached into the envelope and pulled out a magazine. On top was a pale pink square note: *Joyce, Saw this and thought of you. Enjoy! Erin.* I removed the note and there was Keanu Reeves staring at me with his dreamy brown eyes from the cover of *Entertainment Weekly.*

I sprang to my feet, propelling my body to the opening of my cubicle. I waved the magazine above my head. "This is the best day ever," I announced.

My coworkers emerged from their work areas, no doubt to see what it was that had me so invigorated. I was dancing around and jumping up and down as I stared at the image of my idol, ignoring the eye rolling of my coworkers. I pretended not to hear their snickers, moans and groans. Their mocking of my obsession made it even more wonderful.

My phone was ringing again and I stretched my arm into my workstation to grab it. My gaze stayed fixed on Keanu. "Education. Joyce." I said into the receiver.

"Joy."

"Yeah."

"I've been calling all morning."

"I told you I had class." I tried to sound annoyed at the interruption. He didn't need to know I had a video teaching my students while I was enjoying myself.

"I really hate to tell you this over the phone but I have some bad news."

I glanced at the clock. The only thing he had to do that morning before going into the office was to take our children to school. My mind immediately went to reports of missed assignments or petty arguments with classmates. I waited to hear the word *detention* in his next sentence.

But there was no mention of our children in his next statement. "Renee's dead." His voice was shaking and I could tell he was starting to cry.

I froze. The blood in my veins stood still. No air was moving in or out of my lungs. Then I thought about the last time I saw his first cousin, Renee. She'd looked thinner than usual. She told us that she was having problems with her stomach and was going for some testing. I wondered if perhaps something had gone wrong.

The saliva in my mouth was completely dried up so all I managed to get out was a feeble "What?"

"She was shot."

"Oh, my God." I was shaking. The magazine cover was blurring. "Oh, my God!" I yelled. "What?" came out of my mouth again.

A mental picture of Renee at the pharmacy counter in her white lab coat passed before my eyes. A robbery? Someone wanting drugs? A drive-by? I might have been asking these questions out loud but I wasn't sure.

"I don't know," my husband replied. "Aunt Alice got the call after eleven last night and they asked her to come identify the body."

"Oh, my God!"

"She was with the police all night. She called my mother after six this morning. I don't know anything else."

"I can't believe this!"

"Do you want me to come there?"

"No. No. No. I'm okay." I hung up, still clutching the magazine.

"Sit down," someone said. I looked up to see my three coworkers surrounding me in my cubicle. The mauve cloth walls seemed to be closing in.

"What happened?" one of them asked as they forced me to a sitting position in my chair.

I tried to focus but their faces were blank circles and their voices were white noise. One took my hand and removed the magazine from my clutch.

"What's going on?" Nellie asked.

I suppose I told them what I knew, but I didn't know what was coming out of my mouth at the time. I couldn't even recall how I managed to get away from the fortress they formed around me. I didn't know what I was saying to the staff when I returned to the CPR class. All I remember was fuzzy images of faces. Some had mouths agape. Others had their hands clasped over their mouths. There were expressions: Fear. Concern. Confusion. I wasn't sure.

Without any recollection of bridging events, I was being shown to the door by my boss, who was telling me to take all the time I needed. I had my coat on and I was suddenly alone in my car.

I was driving. I came to a stop at the intersection of Lee Park Avenue and Division Street. The looming shadow of St. Al's Church came over my car like a shelter and suddenly funereal images flashed in my head. I saw black dresses and dark suits carrying a casket. I pictured Renee inside. I imagined my husband's aunt and uncle and cousins weeping as men loaded the casket into the back of a hearse.

It was as though I were transforming from a solid state to a liquid one. A chemical reaction was going on inside of me. Liquid was flooding out of my eyes and pouring down my cheeks until I had to squint to see between the tears. It felt like I was looking through my windshield into a hurricane.

Somehow I found my way home. As I got there, the numbness that had taken over my body left. It was like waking from anesthesia. Everything hurt. My heart was beating so hard I thought it might be bruising my breastbone. Breathing was a conscious effort. Respirations were replaced with gasping. The blood pulsed through my veins so hard it was making my arms and legs ache. My head was throbbing along with the beat of my heart. *Ba da da dum dum. Ba da da dum dum. Ba da da dum dum.*

I was shaking when I reached for the phone. It rang a few times before my sister-in-law answered. Her voice was forcefully steady as she said "Hello."

"Camille?"

I think she said my name. I heard her crying. "I'm so glad you're not at work." I told her.

"I couldn't stay there."

"Do you want me to come and get you and bring you here to my house?"

"I'd rather drive myself." Her voice sounded bland and tired. She had been crying so much there was nothing left inside of her.

"Are you sure?"

"Yes. I'll be there in a little while."

"Take your time."

As I waited, I tried to keep busy by rehearsing what I would say. She and Renee were first cousins. They'd grown up together.

Instead my mind went back to the last time I'd been with Renee. It was September and we were at a wedding in Chicago. Camille wasn't able to attend since she was busy planning her own wedding, which was just seven months away. Renee and I were both going to be attendants in Camille's wedding. We were taking notes on everything at the Chicago wedding so we could report back to Camille. And since I was to be Camille's matron-of-honor, I was anxious to talk to Renee about plans for Camille's bridal shower and bachelorette party.

I tried to push the memories of my last encounter with Renee out of my head. I tried to get focused. I needed to get my act together so I could support my sister-in-law. After all, I was a nurse. I had to be strong for everyone else. At least that's what I told myself. But when Camille arrived at my home, we both broke down into tears.

We sat at the kitchen table and cried so long and so hard that after a few hours, there was no water left. We thought about opening a bottle of wine and drinking ourselves into oblivion but knowing that her son and my three children would be home from school soon deterred us. Besides, we both knew that the reality of Renee's sudden death would still be there when we sobered up.

Camille's blond hair was pulled tight into a ponytail, calling attention to her brown eyes that were now lost in circles of red. I'm sure I looked just as spent as I fell back to my numb state. My sister was going to the school to pick up my children and Camille's son. She would drop them off at my house. They were old enough to know things weren't following their normal course for the day and we would need to tell them the news as soon as they came home.

I was elected to do the talking since I'm the nurse. I was always elected to do things people thought were natural to nurses. But at the moment, I didn't feel like a nurse. I felt like a family member. I felt the personal loss. There was no way to distance myself. I reminded myself that I'd informed people of deaths before. I was supposed to know how, yet I found myself having to go through the rules in my head. State the death as fact. Keep it simple. Stay calm. Don't cry.

The door opened and the children came rushing in. "What's wrong?" my nephew Nick asked. His complexion was paler than usual.

He and my children stared at Camille and me with bright eyes. I suppose they were wondering why my sister had picked them up from school and why they were all being brought to my house instead of going to their grandmother's like they usually did after school. And I'm sure they sensed the fragile emotional state Camille and I both were in.

State the death as fact. Keep it simple. Stay calm. Don't cry. I asked them all to have a seat around the table.

The grating of the chairs on the floor echoed in my head as they rushed to get seated. They didn't seem to mind the thunder they were creating. Their attention remained fixed on me.

"Your cousin Renee died last night." It was all I could manage to say.

They looked at each other and then at me. Their eyes were wide. "Why?" my son asked.

I tried not to look back at them. I thought that if I didn't see the confused looks it would be easier to handle. "We don't know. It was an accident." I didn't want to scare them by talking about a shooting. I didn't want them to be as horrified as I was. As a mother, I made this feeble attempt to preserve their innocence.

"What kind of accident?"

"Where is she?"

"Is Aunt Alice here?"

They were firing questions at me - questions I didn't want to answer. Questions I couldn't answer. I'd stated the death as fact. I was trying to keep it simple. It was hard to stay calm. I wanted to cry.

"I don't know" was the only answer I could offer. It is still the only answer I can offer. To this day, it seems surreal. There was nothing simple about it. It was complicated.

Stay calm? I couldn't be calm. Angry. Confused. Depressed. If I appeared calm, it must have meant I'd gone numb again.

Years of investigation since have still left questions. No one knows why Renee was where she was when she was murdered. No one knows who pulled the trigger or why. Everything is still a mystery. A cold case.

I look at my own children, who are now around the same age Renee was when her life was ended. Murder scares me. I lie in bed and battle my memories, and my fears.

But I'm a nurse. I know what I'm supposed to do: State the death as fact. Keep it simple. Stay calm. Don't cry.

Renee's death is a fact, but the circumstances surrounding it aren't simple. It's not easy to stay calm when I think of her, or of murder in general.

Don't cry, I tell myself. Don't cry.

* * *

I wish solving a real murder was like it's depicted on TV. In one hour, including commercials, everything falls into place.

An investigator notices a fragment of flesh in the carpet. He picks it up with tweezers and bags it. A forensic technician runs the DNA and tells the cops something unique about the killer. Maybe he has some rare genetic marker. The database reveals only five people with it live in the state. Only one lives in that city. The police put a tail on him and the suspect leads them to the murder weapon. He confesses and the jury finds him guilty.

Wouldn't that be nice?

We waited while She passed
It was a narrow time
Too jostled were Our Souls to speak
At length the notice came

– from "The Last Night That She Lived" by Emily
Dickinson

Seventeen
DANCE OF DENIAL:
The Struggle of Being a Nurse and a Friend

After fifteen years as a hospital-based nurse educator, I decided to make a change. I took a position at Wilkes University as Director of the Nursing Learning Resource Center. It was exciting. I had my own office and a secretary I didn't have to share with a host of others. I was physically removed from the hospital. And perhaps, I hoped, that would physically remove me from death.

But despite my leaving the bedsides of the dying, Death still found her way into my life. Regardless of the number of experiences I'd had and the years of nursing I'd put in, it seemed I never got much better at dealing with it.

I'd developed coping mechanisms to deal with death and dying during those years, but they now controlled me more than I controlled them. It was an incident at the university that finally made me realize how much we all rely on these learned behaviors to get through the times we think we'll never get through.

During my second year in the academic setting, the department chairperson had hired another RN to help me out in the Nursing Learning Resource Center. Her name was Maggie.

We'd had a busy day, and after a flurry of students in the afternoon, I was happy to sit for a moment and clear my head. I picked up a magazine and read about the latest scandals of the stars. These were hardly earth shattering, but that was the point. Pointless trivia about celebrities was a nice switch from the seriousness of teaching student nurses how to start IVs and administer chemotherapy drugs through central venous catheters.

After an article or two, I strolled to Maggie's office. She too was reading at her desk.

"What are you reading?" I pulled out a chair across from her.

"An article on neurological cancers." She flipped a page and crossed one leg over another. The chair swiveled a bit.

"Egad! I was reading about Jennifer Lopez and the Olsen twins. They're all doing fine, in case you were wondering."

Maggie didn't laugh. She closed the journal and centered it in front of her. "My mom was just diagnosed," she added without taking her eyes off the image of the human brain that graced the cover.

An odd feeling came over me. Not shock or sadness, more like the feeling you get when you flip on a light switch and nothing happens. I wanted to flip the switch again, as though the answer were a fluke and I needed to try again. But after a few seconds, I said, "I'm sorry to hear that." The words seemed lame, but they were all I could manage. "How is she doing?"

"Oh she's good. I'm going to take her shopping today after work. The holidays are coming up and if she starts chemo I don't know how much she'll be able to get around." Maggie continued to leaf through the medical journal, but her eyes never focused.

She was in denial. I knew by her casual tone and matter-of-fact responses that she hadn't fully absorbed the seriousness of her mother's diagnosis.

"Does she drive?" I tried to be casual as well.

"No. My dad usually takes her."

I've thought a lot about that conversation. I've wondered if there were something else I should have said or done. Held her hand, or given her a hug. But for lack of any better idea of how to show I cared, I proceeded the same way I'd begun.

"How's your mom doing?" I asked Maggie each day at work.

Her reply always started with the same word: "Good."

"How's your mom doing?"

"Good. She had all of her scans and blood work."

"How's your mom doing?"

"Good. Her counts are good so they're starting chemo in a couple of days."

"How's your mom doing?"

"Good. I'm going to take some groceries over so she has them for the weekend."

Good. Good. Good. I doubted it really was *good* but felt unable to do anything more than ask. And Maggie seemed unable to answer any other way. In fact, I noticed she even had a hard time talking about it. Her replies always came out as though they weren't answers at all, but rather thoughts she had mistakenly said aloud.

And she seemed to keep herself engaged in some displacement activity whenever the conversation turned to her mother's cancer. She would straighten up her desk, log onto her computer, check e-mails.

"How's your mom holding up?"

"She's good." Maggie focused on the computer screen while her hand moved the mouse around the small black and white cow-print mouse pad.

"How are *you* holding up?"

"Oh, me. I'm good. Wow. An e-mail from Human Resources. They finally processed my paperwork."

I took that as an *I'd like to change the subject now*, and obliged. But I couldn't stop caring about my friend and her mother. And my questions were the only way I knew to show that I cared.

"How'd your mom do with chemo?" I asked a few weeks later when we sat down for lunch at the table in Maggie's office.

"Good." Maggie opened the Styrofoam container and fussed with her sandwich. "She did well with the chemo. I'm going to take her for blood work before I come into work on Friday. I've decided to have Christmas dinner at my house this year. No use having her trying to do all of that."

"She normally does dinner?"

"It's only her and my father and me and my husband and my daughter. It's not much. We don't have to have anything elaborate. I was thinking, a ham. What do you do for the holidays?"

Yet another change-the-subject moment. But I didn't want to push her. She had to deal with her mother's imminent death in her own way. And truth be told, I don't know if I would have done any better. So as usual, I indulged Maggie's desire to change the subject and waited a few weeks before asking again. It seemed that there was a line drawn between showing concern and delving too deep. I walked that line as though it were a high wire.

"How are your mom's counts?"

"Good. A little low, but she's good. I took her some food yesterday." Maggie organized the paperwork piled on the corner of her desk. "I don't want her going shopping with a low white count. Stores are so crowded and everyone's got the flu. How're your kids?"

"So far, so good. They had the flu shot, so I'm hoping they stay healthy. How about your daughter?"

"She's good. What school do your kids go to again?"

The switch-a-roo. With each week, Maggie was getting better at it. Whenever she didn't want to talk, she changed the subject to something more palatable. It was a common coping mechanism that we nurses referred to as "avoidance".

"How were your holidays?"

"Good. How about yours?"

"Fine. Busy though. Aren't they always?"

Maggie nodded.

"How's your mom?"

"She's good. I made dinner for Christmas and took it to her house. We all ate there. It was nice."

"I thought everyone was coming to your house. Was everything okay?"

"Oh yeah. I just thought it would be better instead of making my father drive. And this way my mom could relax and spend Christmas in her own house. It's more traditional to have it there anyway."

"Of course. That was a good idea to take the food there. When's your mom's next chemo treatment? How many did she have so far?"

"She had two. I don't know if they'll do any more. Her counts get too low and she gets sick."

"Will they do anything else? Surgery or anything?"

"No. She's good. They'll just keep monitoring her."

"And how are you?"

"I'm good."

"Do you need any time off? Is there anything you need to do for your mom?"

"No, thanks. We're all doing well."

"Okay. But if you need to come in late or leave early or anything, just let me know."

"Thanks, but I'm good."

I wasn't sure whom Maggie was trying to convince: me or herself. But I didn't stop asking just in case she would one day break down the fortress she was building around herself.

"How was your mom's blood work this month?"

"Good. We'll know more next week. She's going for an MRI."

The conversations became like a well-rehearsed dance. Two steps forward. One step back. Two forward. One back. And step, two, three. And left, two, three. And right, two, three. Maggie and I made our way around the floor, always ending up right back where we started.

"How was the MRI?"

"Good."

"Is the cancer less present?"

"No. She's very weak though. I'm going to go shopping to get her some groceries and things."

"Her appetite's good?"

"No. She hardly eats. She had some pudding yesterday."

"Is it okay that she's not eating?"

"She's good. Do you like chocolate pudding? I should make some and bring it in."

Could chocolate pudding cure cancer? I restrained myself from asking such a ridiculous question, but I wondered if perhaps Maggie needed to be shocked out of the dreamland of denial.

Of course, I didn't really want to be the one to shock her, so when the day came that she brought her pudding in to work, I graciously accepted it.

"Thanks for the dessert, Maggie. It was really good. Did you make some for your mom too?"

"No. Not this time. She hasn't really been eating and my father wouldn't eat chocolate pudding if his life depended on it."

"How could someone not like chocolate?"

We laughed more to break the tension than because the question was funny.

"Your mom's still not eating? Will she have to go to the hospital for IVs if she doesn't eat?"

"No. She's good. The doctor is going to have a nurse from hospice come to see her."

"Hospice?" The word rang inside my head so sharply it was as if I stood too close to the belfry. I knew Maggie's mother was dying. I'd known it the minute she'd told me the diagnosis. But, somehow I didn't expect the time to come so fast. I swallowed the lump in my throat. "Do you need some time off?"

"No. I'm good."

Good. Good? You can't possibly be good! I restrained myself from screaming these words and grabbing Maggie by the shoulders to shake her out of her oblivion. How could I force her to face reality when I myself was having trouble doing it? And it wasn't even my mother who was dying.

I gave her a few days of reprieve from my incessant questions before resuming my inquiries. They were all I had, after all. Questions were the only way I could find to communicate with my friend. Matter-of-fact questions. Just like her matter-of-fact answers.

"Anyone from hospice come to talk to you yet?"

"Oh yeah. It went well. A nurse is going to come every morning to help out. And I go over after work and cook and do whatever."

"Is your mom eating?"

"No. But my dad isn't used to taking care of himself yet."

"How's he doing with all this?"

"He's good. He just needs some, well, some, um, guidance. He never cooked or anything."

"He's lucky to have you."

"Thanks."

A comment. I was glad that I'd been able to make a comment. It wasn't a question. It was a small breakthrough. Very small, but it felt good to be able to say something. Too bad I couldn't keep it up.

On our next encounter, I was right back to questions. "Is hospice working out?"

"Yes. It's good. They come every day and get my mom washed up."

"Does she get out of bed?"

"No. She isn't awake."

"How is that for you?"

"Oh, me? I'm good. I'm going to go over later to check on my dad."

"How's he doing?"

"He's good."

At six months to the day since the first conversation, the call came in. "My mom died this morning. I'm going to take my dad to the funeral director today, but I'll come in to work tomorrow. The funeral isn't until Friday."

I'd known the news would come, but I still felt unprepared. "Please don't feel the need to come to work. Take the week off."

"I'm good. I can work if you need me."

"I don't need you. I'm fine. You need the time off. Stay home and cry."

"Oh, I'm good. But thanks."

I hung up and retreated to my office. This dance of denial was one I myself had danced many times too. Two steps forward. One step back. And step, two, three. And left, two, three. And right, two, three.

You always end up right back where you started.

All over bouquets of roses,
O death, I cover you over with roses and early lilies

– from "When Lilacs Last in the Dooryard Bloom'd" by
Walt Whitman

Eighteen
POWERLESS:
Reminders of Being Human

When I made the decision to move to academia after twenty years of hospital-based nursing, I was excited about working with students. It was a chance to affect the future of nursing. And I'll admit, it was nice to have an office with windows and a secretary who wasn't covering twenty other departments.

I set up my office so my desk was next to one of the windows. When I'd get tired of looking at screens of Power Point lectures and e-mails, I would just look to my left and stare out the window.

It was a nice view. The branches of a tall oak tree shaded my window. It tempered the sun and looked like a giant starburst canopy in the fall.

On many occasions, I would need a break from paperwork and screens. I would swivel my chair to face the outdoors and watch squirrels scurry up and down the trunk of the enormous oak and across the patches of green grass.

They were diligent in their labors. As I took a break from my work, I watched through the glass as they took acorns up to some secret storage facility high in the trees. Most days, their intense regimen would guilt me out about turning my back on my assignments. I would let out a loud sigh and return my attention to the piles of papers that covered my desk.

As time went on, I made up names for the squirrels. Then, for some reason, I began calling all of them Cory. I would watch one of the Corys take off across the lawn, lunge toward the oak tree and spiral around the trunk. I would pull myself away from the window and remark to my secretary how exhausting it would be to have a job like Cory and we would laugh.

It got to be a joke between us when we had a daunting task before us. "We're going to have to work like Cory," one of us would say.

After a year or two of joking about the squirrels, they were dear to us. When I would walk across campus and one would run across my path, I would laugh. When I was in a bad mood or feeling overwhelmed, seeing the squirrels execute their tireless acorn-gathering rituals would make me pause and smile.

One day late in the fall semester, I was striding across campus from my car to my office. My mind was preoccupied with the end of the semester. There were so many activities and reports. I was making a mental to-do list.

I was turning to go up the entrance steps in front of my building when I spied Cory perched on a stump on the other side of the street. I stopped and laughed as I thought about the tasks before me as a pile of acorns I needed to carry one by one to the top of a tree.

As I giggled, I thought about Cory taking a break from the rigor of his job. I pictured him sitting at a construction site with a little hard hat and lunch pail, sipping coffee and making his own to-do list. It was just then I saw Cory jump through the hedges and over the sidewalk. He tried to cross the road to the side I was on.

No! I wanted to scream but couldn't. The traffic light on the corner changed to green. Stop! I wanted to tell him but the words didn't come out. Cory leapt off the curb and between two parked cars. His gray fuzzy body landed on the pavement of the roadway.

WHAM! A blue car came barreling down the street. First the front wheel thumped over him, then the rear wheel.

I gasped. The cold air I inhaled tingled in my chest but I couldn't exhale it. I felt sickened as the grayish-toned lump of fur convulsed on the pavement. His tail stood erect as it shook above the crimson puddle where his head should have been.

I was a nurse. I felt as though I should do something. But standing there in the cold, I was helpless. I had no emergency equipment. I had no medications to give. I wanted to dart out into the street and stay with him in his last moments, but oncoming traffic didn't agree. Cars zipped by. One after the other they made small thuds over Cory and I reluctantly left the scene and went on to my office.

As I ran up the stairs, I thought that perhaps I should get a box to use as a coffin. I could scoop Cory's body off the street and bury him in the yard behind my building. In my office, I didn't even bother to take off my coat. I ran over to the window and looked down.

The traffic light had turned red and the cars had stopped. I stared down at the spot where Cory had used to be. But all that was left was a smear of brownish red and black. No fuzzy gray and taupe. No little black eyes. Cory was nothing more than a hint of drab color on the macadam.

I stood by the window feeling defeated. I reminded myself that it was just a squirrel, but somehow I still felt helpless. It was then that it occurred to me that it wasn't the death of a squirrel that was bothering me. Cory was not just a squirrel – he was Mrs. N, Miss Z and Mr. Healey. He was Ruby and Angela. He was Johnny, Candace, and Renee. Cory was not just a squirrel. He was a reminder that I am powerless against death.

Nineteen
LIFE CHANGING:
Using Death to Rewrite the Past

Did you ever hear a person talk about another individual and wonder how much of what was being said was true, how much flat-out false, and how much was convoluted?

Working in a university setting, I was in contact with young adults on a daily basis. Many of the young women were in relationships. They talked about their boyfriends constantly, so my coworkers and I usually knew all of the boys' names. These students also used social media to let everyone know all about their significant other.

We often joked that when we saw daily posts about how wonderful the boyfriend was we knew the breakup was inevitable. It does seem as though when things aren't going well, a person needs to say positive things over and over. My theory was that they were repeating it not only to convince everyone around that their relationship was good but more so to convince themselves.

For example, Bailey was dating Dan. The campus is small so we heard chatter Dan was partying without her and had been seen with other females at off-campus events. Bailey posted on Facebook or Twitter several times a day.

My boyfriend is so sweet. He brought me a coffee to our morning class. #bestboyfriendever #danismyman #luvu4evah

My coworkers and I shared a laugh. "Looks like Bailey and Dan are headed for a breakup."

A few days later, Bailey came to class crying. She then began to post negative comments on Facebook. *Cheaters never win. Karma is a Bitch #notafanofdan*

Then she posted a picture of a broken heart followed by a series of inspirational quotes. *What doesn't kill us makes us stronger. It takes a strong heart to love. One door closes so a better one can open.*

It's funny how people can use their words to make things appear different than they really are.

* * *

Have you ever gone to a funeral and heard a negative eulogy?

"Dearly beloved, we are gathered here today to celebrate the death of Peter. We are all better off without the son of a bitch in our lives. We hope the bastard rots in hell."

Think about it. No matter how nasty, evil or abusive a person is in life, when he dies people tend to focus on the good. Just as they can use social media to misrepresent or remodel the present, they can use death as an opportunity to recreate the past.

* * *

In school I, like everyone else, took science courses along with nursing courses. Classes on anatomy and physiology were necessary so we could understand the pathophysiology of the diseases we would see in our clinical practice. Chemistry helped us understand how our bodies regulate substances like electrolytes, vitamins and oxygen.

Nursing isn't just about the physical being of a person. It's also about the psyche, environment, and social support. The paradigm of nursing includes four concepts: the nurse, the person (patient), the environment, and health. And according to the mother of our profession, Florence Nightingale, health is not limited to physical health. So, we were also required to take classes in the social and behavioral sciences.

At the time, I didn't quite see why they were important. It wasn't until I was caring for a victim of bullying that I saw the value of understanding social constructs. And it wasn't until I was trying to care for someone who was cutting herself that I realized the manifestations of psychological trauma and emotional pain.

I took Psychology and Sociology during the summer session. The classes were held one after the other in a small classroom in our nursing building. Sociology was first, starting at 9 a.m. and Psychology followed after a short break. We would then get lunch before spending the afternoon sitting through nursing courses, like Pharmacology.

The classroom was too warm and too dim. There was no air conditioning and the shades were kept down to shut out more heat from the glaring sun. I would have preferred to be at home in the pool, so often my mind wandered. I would wonder what my friends who didn't have to take summer classes were doing. I was sure they weren't waking early and having to listen to a monotonous lecture on subcultures.

One class in which my mind never seemed to wander was psychology. The professor, Dr. R, worked hard to hold our attention. He was funny and told jokes throughout the class time. He would often tell us stories to help us understand and remember important concepts. It never felt like he was lecturing us. It was more like we were having a huge conversation in which we could all share stories.

Dr. R talked about grief and the way the mind tried to cope with loss. He talked about how people adapt to the changes they experience in their lives due to the loss. He shared a story with us about his parents.

First he told us about his mother. According to his story, they were close. He'd often gone to her for advice and support. But she'd suffered a massive heart attack and died shortly after he received his baccalaureate degree. He wasn't much older when she died than we were at the time we were taking his class. He asked us how we would feel if we got a call that one of our parents had died suddenly.

I didn't even want to think about that.

Many of the students shared stories about personal experiences. Others asked questions. I didn't contribute to the discussion that ensued.

"Did you get to the hospital in time to see your mom before she died?" one of the students asked Dr. R.

He told us he had not.

The student who had asked this said she would be upset if that happened. She said she would want to say her goodbyes. The rest of the class nodded.

The professor told us it didn't bother him. He explained that he was sad about his mother's death and that he'd gone through a period of grieving. He even told us he still missed her. He joked that he didn't know how to coordinate his outfits since she died and that was why we would often see him in mismatched clothes. (That day, he was wearing a navy and white gingham checked shirt with khaki pants and a red and yellow striped tie.)

What struck me as odd was that he wasn't upset he hadn't gotten to see his mom one last time before she died.

Didn't he want to tell her he loved her and that he was going to miss her?

He said he wasn't upset because he was content with the relationship he'd had with her during life. He'd told his mother he loved her every time he saw her. He said he was certain he'd told her so as they ended their very last telephone conversation.

"Sadness, yes. But no regrets," he said.

I'd always assumed the closer I was to a person, the harder it would be to accept his or her death. According to Dr. R, that was not strictly true. If we were content with the relationship when he or she was alive, we would be content when he or she died.

This piqued my interest.

He went on to tell us that he still talked to his mother. He even claimed she sometimes answered him.

"You mean like in dreams?" a student asked.

He said yes, sometimes she came in dreams, but at other times he would picture her sitting in a chair or standing in the kitchen at his childhood home and he would hear her voice.

"A ghost?"

He laughed and told us he didn't believe in ghosts. Then he went on to talk about how our minds can preserve our memories and our relationships even after the death of a loved one. He said that the dead were still with us in the memories and that those could be so powerful we could still see our loved ones vividly and hear their voices as clearly as if they were physically present.

I was on the edge of my seat.

He also told us that after someone dies, people tend to only remember the good memories. It's as if death gives them an opportunity to rewrite the past.

He shared with us a story about his father. A few years after Dr. R's mother's death, his father remarried. Dr. R joked that his perception of his father's second wife was that she was a wicked stepmother from a fairy tale. He kidded that the reason he went to California to get his Masters degree was so he would be far away from her. He said her cooking was awful and he was afraid she might have been trying to poison him. I wasn't sure if she was really as mean as he was portraying her or if he was just trying to amuse us with exaggerations. He did love to make us laugh. He said even his father would confide to him sometimes that he should never have remarried.

Dr. R did sound sympathetic when he explained that after a few years of marriage, his stepmother developed cancer. It wasn't diagnosed until after it had metastasized, spread to other organs, and she was very sick and in a lot of pain at the end of her life.

Although his father was unhappy in his second marriage, things changed after the second wife died. Dr. R told us that his dad began talking about Number Two non-stop – and every story had a positive spin.

"I witnessed most of the events my father was sharing and knew his stories weren't accurate," Dr. R told us before continuing with one to serve as an example.

Dr. R's sister had had a baby girl she named after their late mother. The family was ecstatic and his father was proud to welcome his first grandchild. The stepmother refused to attend the baptism. Instead she stayed home and complained to her husband that his family made her feel left out. This led to an argument and his father spent a few nights at his son's apartment because he was tired of being blamed and berated.

"But then," he went on, "after she died, the story changed!" His father's new version was that his second

183

wife didn't go to the baptism because she didn't feel well and that she felt awful for having to miss it.

"Do you see what he did there? He rewrote the memory!" Dr. R was animated so I laughed along with my classmates.

While I remembered this, I never quite understood it until many years later. Having lost numerous family members and close friends to death, I've noticed how I remember the deceased, as well as how others remember them. And the memories do seem to get a fresh coat of paint as the years go by.

* * *

I didn't know Mary Jean and John until they were in their fifties. It was the 1980s and when I met them, they'd already been married over twenty-five years. From the time we got acquainted, I could never understand why they were married to each other. They didn't seem to have anything in common, and they never did anything together. They acted more like disgruntled roommates than husband and wife. I wondered if their parents had had this type of relationship and so they thought it was normal. Maybe their religious beliefs had them convinced they had no alternative. Perhaps it was just easier to stay together than to file for divorce. They did seem to have worked out a system where they rarely if ever had to see each other.

He lived his own life: working long hours, hanging out with his friends and hiding money from his wife. She lived hers: shopping, going to the gym, spending her off time with her coworkers. Their interactions were far from loving. He would speak and she would roll her eyes and point out to everyone in earshot how terrible he was. "I'm going straight to heaven for having to deal with him," she would say. He would grumble under his breath and call her a bitch.

At first I was uncomfortable but after a while I got used to it and just chuckled when either would complain to me about the other.

They rarely did anything together in all the years I knew them. And I knew them for nearly thirty years. They were married for over fifty years and had lived into their late seventies. Then one day John died.

After his death, Mary Jean began talking about her late husband non-stop. He would have said this. He would have done that.

Like Dr. R's father, she started sharing memories that had been edited. Heavily. "We used to have so much fun at the shore." (No they didn't. He would never leave the hotel room and would complain incessantly about everything.) "When we got lost while driving to New Jersey, we laughed so hard." (No one had laughed. They'd both been angry and had blamed each other for not getting better directions. They were so angry, neither of them ate when the family stopped for dinner on the route home). "When John met the mayor, he was so excited." (No he wasn't. He'd complained and made inappropriate comments that embarrassed everyone.)

His birthday became a mandatory family holiday and visiting his grave a weekly ritual. Death allowed her to rewrite the past. She was no longer burdened with him but saddened by the loss. I wondered if they'd ever had a relationship like the one she was now portraying. Perhaps they had once, long ago, in the years before I knew them. But it seemed unlikely.

Mary Jean isn't the only one I've seen do this. I hear survivors tell stories over and over about the dead - each version edited more than the last – adding positive and deleting negative. And it isn't limited to husbands and wives, family members and close friends. This rewriting of the past isn't only done by the old. The young do it too.

A group of teenage girls were at a local bazaar (what we call church picnics in Northeastern Pennsylvania). Four or five of them were sitting at the end of one of the picnic tables under a white and yellow striped tent. They'd most likely spent the afternoon coordinating their outfits. They wore denim cutoffs so short the pocket linings were hanging out from below the frayed edges. Each wore a tight V-neck t-shirt with a brand name across the front and matching flip-flops. Their lips were shining bright with lip gloss.

I'd just exited the food tent and was scanning for an empty seat, where I could eat. When I saw the girls, they were huddled at one end of a picnic table, so the other end was vacant. I sat down at the empty end. They didn't seem to notice. They were busy gossiping about a classmate. I knew a few of the girls since I was a member of the congregation hosting the bazaar and they and their families were as well. Sunday after Sunday, I'd watched them grow from infants to toddlers, from tweens to teens.

They were all talking as though they were one person. It was hard to tell which girl said what but as I enjoyed my potato pancakes I had nothing better to do than eavesdrop. It was hard not to. They were talking loudly, and their voices joined, sounding like one long run-on sentence.

"Bradley's so lame. He tells everyone he hangs out with us and I'm like, um, no he doesn't. We do *not* even talk to *him*. Ew. Seriously, he is uber lame. I don't even look at him cuz my eyes would probably burn he's so gross. Remember when he asked me to the semi? Yea right, like I would seriously be caught dead with him. Who did he even go with? I think Kirsten. Figures, she's a loser too."

The boy they were speaking of took his life a few months later. I knew his parents, so I went to the funeral service. The school provided his classmates with a bus so they could leave their classes that day and attend the memorial.

The church was filled to capacity. From my seat near the back, I spotted the same girls who'd been at the bazaar. They were huddled together crying and consoling each other throughout the service. On the way out of the church I could hear them talking. "Bradley was so sweet. I can't believe he's gone. Why did he kill himself? I wish he would have just called someone to talk."

I wanted to slap them, but remembered Dr. R's class. They needed to rewrite the past. They needed to convince themselves everything was good between them and the deceased boy. They would most likely continue saying these things over and over for years.

When I look at old pictures, I see many friends who've since died. I think about them and their survivors. I think back to the things people said when they spoke about them in life. In some cases, I'm still close with the survivors, so I hear the stories now being shared about the dead. In other cases, I've lost touch, and can only wonder how those still here are remembering those who have gone.

Sometimes I see posts on social media. *I miss my mom. Happy birthday in heaven, dad. #loveugramma.* I wonder what the real relationships were like.

Death physically takes people from us in this life, but it cannot take away our memories. It does give us a chance to edit the past - an opportunity to fix our broken relationships with the deceased. Death allows us to cover up our guilt and regret with more pleasant versions of what happened.

Is this a good thing? A bad thing? I think neither, really. It's a coping mechanism that allows us to go on with our lives. At times, death offers the opportunity to reshape the past into something we can live with. We can cover the bad memories with bright fresh paint. We can remodel our guilt and resentments into an acceptable version of our life with the deceased. We can throw away the words we wish we hadn't said, the actions we wish we hadn't done, and convince ourselves none of it happened. Then we can focus on the departed the way we wish they'd been, or the way we wish we'd been to them.

And if our relationship was good, we can continue it after death. Through memories and moments we cherish, we can keep our loved ones with us in spirit. They can live on through us each time we share a story or a post about them on social media:

A post of a burning candle with the legend: *Burning this in memory of my father*.

A favorite photo of the deceased. Can't believe it's been ten years.

#YOURENOTDEADTILISAYYOURDEAD

To elaborate is no avail, learn'd and unlearn'd feel that it is so.

Sure as the most certain sure, plumb in the uprights, well entreatyed, braced in the beams,

Stout as a horse, affectionate, haughty, electrical,

I and this mystery here we stand.

Clear and sweet is my soul, and clear and sweet is all that is not my soul.

Lack one lacks both, and the unseen is proved by the seen,

Till that becomes unseen and receives proof in its turn.

— From "Song of Myself" by Walt Whitman

Twenty
PARADISE REVISITED:
Looking Back at Near-Death

In these chapters, I've shared my most memorable experiences with death. I promised to share them openly and honestly, and I hope I have. But there's one very important story I left incomplete.

If I'm going to explore death and my attitudes toward it, it's a story I have to revisit. It is that of my car accident and the out of body experience I had when I was eighteen.

But how can I talk about my own death, or even my own near-death? How can I tell you about my near-death experience without having to confront my own mortality?

I don't know the answer, but I'll try.

In 1983, I demolished my car when I swerved and lost control while trying to avoid a rabbit. I left my body for a brief time and found myself in a beautiful garden.

I was walking in a large open field. The grass beneath me was a blend of the most beautiful shades I had ever seen. It was spotted with patches of vibrantly colored flowers.

I felt wonderful. There was no pain or stress or worry. I was totally free. I loved the feeling and I frolicked through the garden like a child.

There was a path, and I followed it. To my left rose a copse of trees. An awe-inspiring light gleamed beyond them. I ran toward it.

But just before I reached it, a force stopped me. I stood near a rock, staring into the light and listening to the soothing voice of a woman. I couldn't make her words out, but I believed I understood what she was telling me. I knew I needed to listen. Perhaps she was giving me some sort of choice, or telling me my fate, or giving me a warning. But to this day, I have no memory of what she actually said.

Through the years, though, there have been times I felt scared and overwhelmed. When that's happened, I've closed my eyes and let my mind take me back to the garden. I remember the light and feel comforted. I recall that wordless voice, and it gives me confidence to go forward. I can't explain why or how. It just is.

I left the garden. I "went back" to the accident scene, to my earthly life, and in the years since, I've rarely mentioned that garden, that light, or that voice to anyone, ever. Until now.

I kept my vision to myself. But at night, when I was alone in my bed, I asked why. Why was I back here on this earth? I didn't have a logical answer, but I could hear her voice and I knew that here was where I belonged, at least for now.

Now, when I look back at the accident and my time in the garden I wonder why I wasn't afraid. What would I do if the same thing happened to me now? Would I be afraid? Would I go willingly?

Life has changed so much since I was eighteen. Death has taken so many I loved, and life has given me more to love. My family is no longer just parents and sisters. It is children.

Funny, I know more now yet feel like I know less. I seemed to have answers then. Now, I have mostly questions.

I now find myself revisiting memories of death and it seems that She has a penchant for making her presence known to me, as if She doesn't want me to forget about the garden.

As I began writing this book, my grandmother was diagnosed with a terminal illness. Amma, as I called her, was my last living grandparent. It was mid-October when she was taken to the hospital and by the end of the month, we were told her condition was not treatable.

"It's that time of the year," I said when I shared the news of her condition.

Despite my saying this (and knowing this), I was still somewhat shocked when we had to make the decision to have her transferred to a hospice unit. I suppose the denial that came from being a granddaughter outweighed the logic that came with being a nurse.

"How's your grandmother?" friends would ask.

"Oh she's good. She has renal failure."

"How's your grandmother?"

"She's good. She's in the hospice unit."

I danced the dance of denial.

It was a Tuesday around five in the evening. My mother had finally gone home to eat supper. (She'd been at my grandmother's bedside almost continually since her hospitalization.) I sat alone at Amma's side counting her respirations. *Resps = 14* I murmured to myself. I was torn between my roles.

The truth was I couldn't stop being the nurse. I wanted to help her. I had to remind myself that helping her didn't mean keeping her alive. In my heart, I knew that helping her now meant letting her go.

I envisioned the garden and knew she would be happy there. I wondered if she could see it. Amma, can you see the light behind the trees? Isn't it beautiful? Aren't the colors magnificent? Don't you feel weightless and free?

My mind went back into nursing mode. I thought about what I would do if I were her nurse instead of her granddaughter. And I remembered a ritual we used to perform in the ICU.

If a dying patient seemed to be unable to let go, we would make sure that he or she had said goodbye to everyone necessary. Then we would open the window, to set the spirit free. It always seemed to work. We would open the window and tell the patients it was okay to go. They would relax. Their breathing would slow. Then they would exhale, one last time, and their heart would stop. It would be peaceful. Calm. Serene.

I thought about this as I sat there listening to Amma breathe.

She and I had a bond. We were both middle children. When we were together, we would vent our frustrations over our birth order. "In the middle playing the fiddle," she would say. When we were in the company of the family and my mother and sister would be making plans, we would look at each other with our secret smirk. We didn't need to say anything. We understood. "We have to listen to the bosses," she would whisper. And we would laugh. Most of the time, we weren't opposed to their plans. We just liked sharing an inside joke.

Remembering this made me laugh. I stood and turned to the window. I lifted the large white shade. I grasped the dull silver handle and turned it to the left. With the window ajar, I pulled the shade back down to deter the breeze. Then I turned to my grandmother.

"I opened the window, Amma. You can go whenever you want. The bosses aren't here."

The corners of her mouth and eyes curved up into a smirk.

I didn't want to be there when she took that last breath. Maybe I was afraid my inner nurse would force me to try to resuscitate her. Maybe I was just too afraid to feel the pain. I leaned down and kissed her. "Bye, Amma." I left the room and the hospital.

She granted my wish, and didn't draw her last breath with me there. But she did wait for the bosses to be there. She died a couple of hours later. "It was eight twenty," my sister told me when I arrived once again at my grandmother's bedside.

The time didn't matter. After all, what is the *time of death?*" I still wonder about that. I still wonder what it is that defines life and death. I still wonder why it hurts so much when someone dies. And I wonder why it is so hard to let go of the memories and the spirit of those that have died.

My mind drifts back to the garden. I picture those who've have died, laughing and walking in that beauty and peace. I think about my own brief visit there. And I ask myself, What would I do if I were there right now? Would I come back once more? Or choose to go with the light?

I have a feeling that I would pull up to the rock in my car. I'd press a button and my window would whir down. I'd lean out, look into the light and say, there you are, Death. So glad I found you! I have a lot of questions. Maybe this time she would give me an answer I could understand . . . and remember.

What is a man anyhow? what am I? what are you?
All I mark as my own you shall offset it with your own,
Else it were time lost listening to me.

— From "Song of Myself" by Walt Whitman

Postscript:
THE SHROUD

L iving and dying, life and death, and our attitudes about them are part of who we are. Just as each of us is physically different from any other, so are the concepts, experiences and coping mechanisms we carry within us. Our bodies are unique to each of us, as are our spirits.

I picture each human being as a work of art on a loom. Genetics determine the long threads of DNA that stretch up and down the vertical axis. One strand makes me a brunette. Another gives me blue eyes. There's a strand that makes me petite and others that give me long arms and short legs.

It's my experiences that determine the threads of the horizontal axis. Life weaves its threads through me, making its way from end to end as they become part of me: threads of happiness and sadness, pride and shame, passion and apathy, life and death. Throughout life, these threads shape what becomes the one and only me.

What if everyone were a work of art on a loom? We would each have vertical strands that determined our physical characteristics and we would each have the horizontal strands of our experiences. Someone might evolve into a pot holder, a placemat, a rug, a blanket or, a shawl. I would be a shroud.

I shroud myself as a nurse. I am scared and vulnerable, but shroud myself with bravery and confidence. I am helpless before death, but shroud myself with hope.

I've told you the stories of those whose deaths have affected me over the years. I may not have been able to define the "time of death" in scientific terms, but by exploring my experiences with the dying, I have come to understand much more about myself. I understand now that being a nurse is part of who I am and that no matter where I go or what happens to me, I can't NOT be a nurse. I've learned that I cannot control death. However, I have also learned that I will most likely never stop trying. I can now see how my "life with death" has defined and shaped who I am.

I think about death often. Right now, I'm still thinking about my grandmother's passing, and my father's. I realize that the grandmother who used to sew my clothes and my children's clothes is gone. My father, who taught me about joists and band saws, is gone. Their deaths are facts. But the woman who taught me math and empathized with me about being a middle child is still with me. The man who taught me how to be a good parent is still with me. Their spirit will always be with me because they've become part of the fabric of who I am.

Thus, I am who I am in large part because of my experiences with death and dying. So I feel comfortable saying that I am who I am because of the people whose lives and deaths I have explored in this book. These people may be dead in body, but as long as I hold on to their spirit, they are not dead to me. Nothing is ended that is not forgotten. They are very much alive as part of me. And as long as I keep their spirit with me, they will never be dead, until I say they are dead.

End Notes

Brenda Hage, PhD, DNP, CRNP is a professor of nursing and chairperson of graduate nursing programs at Misericordia University in Dallas, Pennsylvania. She is the NEPA Vice Chairperson of POLST (Physician Orders for Life-Sustaining Treatment). The National POLST Paradigm is a voluntary system that elicits, documents and honors patients' treatment wishes through portable medical orders. A POLST form is based on conversations between patients and health care professionals about goals of care, quality of life, diagnosis, prognosis, and treatment options.

The works of Emily Dickinson and Walt Whitman are in the public domain. Dickinson's are some of the most beautiful poems about death I've ever read. Whitman's, on the other hand, are some of the most depressing. But he was a nurse, so that explains a lot.

Chapter One
Jenny and Greg were main characters on the soap opera *All My Children,* aired on ABC from 1970 to 2011. It was created by Agnes Nixon and set in a fictional Philadelphia suburb called Pine Valley. I began watching it with my father's mother when she used to babysit for me. Gram also let me drink coffee with a tablespoon of sugar and eat crackers with globs of butter.
"Fantasy" was written and recorded by Canadian guitarist and vocalist Aldo Nova, on his self-titled album, *Aldo Nova.* It was produced by Portrait Records (a division of Epic Records) and released in 1982.

Chapter Two
Peanuts was created by Charles M. Schutz in 1950. The Peanuts Gang were first seen in newspaper comics, or "funnies." In 1965, CBS began airing television specials featuring them.
David Cassidy, a 1970s pop icon, catapulted to fame as heartthrob Keith Partridge in *The Partridge Family*. It aired on ABC from 1970-1974. Cassidy continued a singing career after the show ended. His best known song is "I Think I Love You."
Pong was an arcade game released by Atari in 1972. You could only buy it at Sears. My friend was considered to be very lucky to have a home gaming system in 1978.

Chapter Four

On Death and Dying was published by Macmillan, New York, New York in 1969.

The Elisabeth Kübler-Ross Foundation maintains a website with links to her books and to the Kübler-Ross Library at Hospice Atlanta.

On Grief and Grieving: Finding the Meaning of Grief Through the Five Stages of Loss was written by Kübler-Ross with David Kessler (Scribners, New York 2005). Kessler has appeared as an expert on death and dying on *The Oprah Winfrey Show* and *The Dr. Oz Show*.

The Simpsons aired on FOX beginning in 1991. The episode discussed here was written by Nell Scovell. It was titled "One Fish, Two Fish, Blowfish, Blue Fish."

Laws governing pregnancy and termination are regulated by individual states. This leads to differences in how the fetus is handled in different regions of the country. State laws, however, can be greatly influenced by national laws.

Chapter Five

Dark Shadows aired on ABC from 1966 to 1971.

Carrie was written by Stephen King. (Doubleday, 1974).

The Exorcist was directed by William Friedkin and released by Warner Brothers in 1973. The film was based on a novel by William Peter Blatty.

Poltergeist was directed by Tobe Hooper. It is a trilogy first distributed by Metro-Goldwyn-Mayer in 1982. The story was by Steven Spielberg and the screenplay by Steven Spielberg, Michael Grais and Mark Victor (not a relative of mine).

Chapter Six

The *Advanced Cardiac Life Support (ACLS)* textbooks and training materials are produced by the American Heart Association (AHA), Grapevine, Texas. The AHA updates the curricula every five years based on updates in science and technology.

Candid Camera ran from 1948 through 1992. It was created and produced by Allen Funt and Allen Funt Productions.

"Girls Just Wanna Have Fun" was recorded by Cyndi Lauper on her album *She's So Unusual*. It was released by Record Plant, New York, New York, in 1983.

Chapter Seven

Jurassic Park was produced by Amblin Entertainment and released by Universal Pictures in 1993. It was based on the novel *Jurassic Park,* by Michael Crichton.

Medical Center aired on CBS from 1969 through 1976. It was created by Al Ward and Frank Glicksman and produced by MGM Television.

Marcus Welby, MD aired on ABC from 1969 through 1976. The show was created by David Victor (also no relation) and produced by David Victor and David J. O'Connell.

Hot Stuff, officially titled, *Hot Stuff the Little Devil*, was a comic book character created in 1957 by Warren Kremer and published by Harvey Comics. Production continued until the early 1990s.

Archie Comics is a comic book series featuring fictional teenagers. The characters were created in 1941 by publisher, John L. Goldwater artist, Bob Montana, and writer, Vic Bloom. The official *Archie Comics* was founded by Maurice Coyne, Louis Silberkleit and John L. Goldwater and is headquartered in Pelham, New York.

Chapter Eight

ER was a popular show among nurses. Everyone I knew watched it. The show aired on NBC from 1994 through 2009. The specific episode discussed here was written by John Wells III. It was titled "Dead of Winter."

Chapter Ten

The Patient Self-Determination Act (PSDA) of 1990 was introduced by Representative Sander M. Levin, a Democrat from Michigan, and passed the 101st Congress as H.R.4449.

Chapter Eleven

Stiff: The Curious Lives of Human Cadavers is a 2003 non-fiction work by Mary Roach. It was published by W. W. Norton & Company, New York, New York.

Chapter Thirteen

Doug Ross was played by George Clooney on the NBC show *ER,* as noted in the endnotes for Chapter Eight.

"A Christmas Carol" is by Charles Dickens. I had the privilege of seeing it performed as a play at Madison Square Garden with tenor Terrance Mann as Scrooge.

Chapter Fourteen

The *Pediatric Advanced Life Support (PALS)* textbooks and training materials for providers and instructors are produced by the American Heart Association. They are updated every five years.

Broselow Pediatric Emergency Tape, more commonly called the Broselow Tape, is a color-coded tape that provides a quick reference to medical instructions needed when a pediatric patient requires resuscitation. The tape was developed by ER physician James Broselow in the early 1980s. In 1985, Robert Luten of the University of Florida was a member of the American Heart Association's Pediatric Life Support subcommittee. He introduced the tape and it was adopted by the AHA for use in PALS courses and as the recommended standard in pediatric resuscitation efforts.

Chapter Fifteen

Dark Shadows aired on ABC from 1966 to 1971. It is also referenced in Chapter Five.

Hill Street Blues aired on NBC from 1981 through 1987. Steven Bochco and Michael Kozoll were the show's creators. *The Love Boat* aired on ABC beginning in 1977. Aaron Spelling and Douglas Cramer were the executive producers. *Fantasy Island* aired on ABC from 1977 to 1984. It was created by Gene Levitt and produced by Spelling-Goldberg Productions and Columbia Pictures Television.

"Like a Virgin" was recorded by pop artist, Madonna, on her album *Like a Virgin,* released by The Power Station, New York, New York, in 1984.

Adam Ant (Stuart Leslie Goddard) was a punk rock icon in the late 1970s and early 1980s. Based in London, he recorded with CBS, Columbia, MCA, and EMI.

"We Are Family" was recorded by Sister Sledge on their album *We Are Family.* It was released by Cotillion and The Power Station, New York, New York, in 1978.

Freaky Friday was a film released by Walt Disney Studios in 1976. It was directed by Gary Nelson. A remake was released in 2003.

Chapter Sixteen

Dickies is a clothing label founded in Bryan, Texas in 1918. Now headquartered in Fort Worth, they distribute pants, scrubs, and a variety of other products for the healthcare and other industries.

Keanu Reeves, a Beruit-born actor, starred in *Bill and Ted's Excellent Adventure, Speed, The Matrix* trilogy, and more recently, *John Wick*. I developed a crush on him when he played a goalie in *Youngblood*.

Entertainment Weekly was founded by David Morris in 1990. It is published by Time, Inc.

Chapter Seventeen

Jennifer Lopez and the Olsen Twins were actresses popular in the late1990s and early 2000s.

Chapter Nineteen

Facebook, a corporation specializing in social media, was founded in 2004 by Mark Zuckerberg, Dustin Moskovitz, Andrew McCollum, Eduardo Saverin and Chris Hughes.

Twitter is a social networking service founded by Jack Dorsey, Evan Willimas, Biz Stone, and Noah Glass in 2006. Posts on Twitter are referred to as tweets. They use the hash tag as a grouping mechanism. Since tweets are limited to 140 characters, users sometimes don't use spaces between words and often misspell words and use numbers like 2 for the word "to" and 4 for the word "for." #norespect4grammar.

Acknowledgements

I would like to thank my parents, Laverne and the late Eugene Victor, for teaching me the value of hard work and perseverance. I would also like to thank my sisters, Darlene Dubinski and Gayle McCune. Love you!

Thank you to my cousins, Dennis and the late Paul Hiller, who were really more like big brothers. They read to me when they babysat me. The house of books they built for me was awesome!

Special thanks goes out to Sister Felicia Ann, who taught me the basics of writing back in the seventh grade at Holy Trinity School in Nanticoke, Pennsylvania. Dr. Joan Lockhart of Duquesne University and the late Dr. Ashim Basu of Wilkes University encouraged me to publish scholarly articles. Drs. Bonnie Culver and Michael Lennon accepted me into the creative writing community at Wilkes University. My Deans, Drs. Mary Ann Merrigan and Deborah Zbegner, allowed me to balance writing with my nursing and teaching careers. Dr. Melanie Turk at Duquesne encouraged my spirit of inquiry.

Nancy McKinley, my mentor in the Wilkes Creative Writing program, taught me craft and helped me find my voice. Now *I* can say "literature" too! Chris Busa was the first to encourage me to write creative nonfiction, and helped me understand my proclivity for writing about death and dying.

Thanks to all the writers I worked and studied with at Wilkes, especially the Cockeye Book Club. Special thanks to Jim Scheers who walked through a blizzard to see me, spent days reading and editing my work, and encouraged me in the publication process.

Thank you to David Poyer and Lenore Hart of Northampton House Press for publishing so many great works. Your contribution to the writing world is significant. Thanks also to Naia Poyer for creating a cover design that captured not only the essence of this book but also my quirky sense of humor.

Special thanks to Dr. Brenda Hage for writing the Introduction and for fighting for patients' rights, especially when they're at the end of their lives.

Last but most importantly, a huge thank you goes out to my children, Paul John, Bethany and Cornelia. Of all of my accomplishments, being your mom is the greatest. Love y'all.

Northampton House Press

Established in 2011, Northampton House Press publishes selected fiction, nonfiction, memoir, and poetry. Check out our list at www.northampton-house.com, and Like us on Facebook – "Northampton House Press" – as we showcase more innovative works from brilliant new talents.

Made in the USA
Middletown, DE
06 January 2018